Agile Software:
Patterns of Practice

Joseph Bergin, Ph.D.

Agile Software: Patterns of Practice
Joseph Bergin, Ph.D.
Pace University
jbergin@pace.edu

Published by Joseph Bergin, Software Tools, February 2012

Copyright

ISBN 978-0-9851543-2-5

cover design: barbara esmark

Preface

A Bridge to Agile Software Development Practice

This collection of patterns complements and summarize the standard wisdom that can be gleaned from the Agile Development literature such as Kent Beck's *Extreme Programming Explained* or Ken Schwaber and Mike Beedle's *Agile Software Development with Scrum*. It is directed primarily at those who are starting out with Scrum or Extreme Programming (XP) or another agile methodology and might miss some subtle ideas. Once a team gains experience these patterns will become obvious, but initially some of them are counter intuitive. While this study began in Extreme Programming practice, most of the advice applies to agile development in general and Scrum in particular.

I consider XP to be a pattern language in which the practices are the basis of the patterns. They have the characteristics of a true Pattern Language in that they are synergistic and generative. The dozen or so practices detailed in Beck and elsewhere, such as "Do the simplest thing that could possibly work" and "Yesterday's Weather" form a subset of this language.

While I have gathered information from various authors and practitioners as well as my own practice and consulting, I take responsibility for what is said here.

This book presents more than one hundred patterns developed so far. Each of the patterns is described briefly in the Thumbnails section at the end.

The Author

Joseph (Joe) Bergin has been a professor for nearly 40 years, originally in Mathematics, but mostly in Computer Science. He was an early pattern writer and advocate as well as an early adopter of agile software development. He has consulted with large companies who wish to explore agile methods and wonder whether they would find a good fit. Among other things, he is a certified Scrum Master and Coach. He is also an avid practitioner of Tai Chi, a photographer, and a cook.

Web Sites:
http://csis.pace.edu/~bergin
http://jbergin.com
Printed Version of this book:
http://www.cafepress.com/jbergin

How To Use This Book

This is intended as a reference for practitioners "in the trenches." Don't feel like you need to read it from beginning to end, as it isn't intended for that use. Use the Table of Contents to find things of interest to you at the point you are in your process. If you are really new to this, see the advice chapters and the Getting Started with Agile Development chapter. Use the names of the patterns highlighted there, as well as in the Agile Development Story to guide you.

For an individual pattern, first judge whether the stated context matches your own. Then ask if the problem applies to you at that moment. If that is true, consider applying the solution. The forces should help you understand why the solution is the right one, and the commentary should help you understand what to expect next.

Consult the References and the Additional Resources for more on the various aspects of agile development. There is both wisdom and the experience of practice there.

Table of Contents

Copyright...ii
Preface..iii
Agile Software: Patterns of Practice..1
What Are Patterns?..1
What is Agility?...2
Some Key Ideas Explained...3
A Few Abbreviations...8
An Agile Development Story (a.k.a. Fairy Tale)..8
Fundamental Patterns of Agility..11
Sheltering Manager...11
Effective Coach...13
ScrumMaster...15
Onsite Customer (Product Owner)..16
Whole Team..19
Train Everyone...21
One Project..23
Self-Organizing Team...24
Just Start...25
Guiding Metaphor (Topos)..26
Best Effort 28
Sprint...30
Planning Game (Sprint Planning Meeting)...31
Stories (Product Backlog)...32
Initial Velocity..34
High Value First 35
Deliver Customer Value..37
Yesterday's Weather...38
Test First...39
Executable Tests...41
Collective Responsibility..43
Stand Up Meeting (Daily Scrum)...45
Small Releases (Incremental Development)..47
Easy Does It (Don't Push Too Hard)...48
Be Human (Humane Workplace)..50
Sacred Schedule (Sprint) 52
Bug Generates Test...54
Implementer Estimates Task...55
Estimate Whole Task..57

Team Owns Individual Velocities..59

Spike 61

Promiscuous Programming 63

Cards and Whiteboards..65

Documentation Is Just Another Task..67

Question Implies Acceptance Test...69

Re-estimate Periodically..71

Flexible Velocity..73

Once And Only Once..75

Continuous Integration 76

Social Tracker..78

Project Diary..80

Customer Checks-Off Tasks..82

Customer Obtains Consensus...84

Individual Stakeholder Budgets...86

Simple Design (Incremental Design)...87

Coding Standard...88

Collective Ownership (Shared Code)..89

Ask For More...90

Graceful Retreat..91

Do the Simplest Thing That Could Possibly Work (DTSTTCPW)...........92

You Ain't Gonna Need It (YAGNI)...93

Constant Refactoring..94

Negotiated Scope Contract..96

Energized Work...97

Sustainable Pace...99

Pair Programming...100

Common Development Environment..102

End To End..103

Retrospective...104

Test Card..105

Acceptance Tests..106

Informative Workspace (Visible Project Tracker)..................................107

Just Do It..108

Shrinking Teams...109

Ten Minute Build..110

My Story...111

Full Communication...112

Infrastructure..113

 High Discipline...114

Our Space..115
Team Continuity...116
Relative Estimates...117
Half A Loaf..118
Nano-Project..119
Personal Velocity...120
Offer Alternatives 121
Beyond Extreme (Extreme Discipline)..................................122
Agility in Large Systems...123
Think Small..123
Scrum of Scrums..124
Grow Up...125
Interfaces Are Just Another Story 126
Architecture Sprint...127
Agility in Dispersed Development Teams......................................128
Local Manager...128
Kickoff...130
All Manager Scrum..131
Virtual Workspace..132
Multiple Communication Modes..133
Shorten The Path..134
Presence Indicator..135
Grow Out..136
Customer Tester Pair...137
Be Together..138
Face Time...139
Ambassador..140
Remote Pair..141
Single Point Organization...142
Feature Focused Teams...143
Rapid Response Teams..144
Cultural Awareness...145
Bonding 146
Some Speculation...147
Daily Deployment...147
Pay Per Use..148
Clusters of Patterns of Agile Practice 149
Advice For Managers..153
Advice For Customers...155
Advice For Developers 157

Getting Started With Agile Development...158
How Agility Wins..160
Additional Resources..162
Acknowledgements 163
Thumbnails 164
References 170
Index 171

Index of Diagrams

Scrum Patterns...5
Extreme Programming Patterns..7
Sheltering Manager...12
Effective Coach...14
Onsite Customer..18
Whole Team 20
Executable Tests...42
Collective Responsibility 44
Continuous Integration 77
Constant Refactoring...95
Pair Programming..101
Estimate Whole Task Cluster...149
Dispersed Agile Development Cluster..151
Large System Development Cluster..152

Agile Software: Patterns of Practice

Joseph Bergin

What Are Patterns?

Software and Organizational Patterns grew out of the work of Christopher Alexander and others in architecture [1]. Alexander wanted to return to ordinary people the ability to participate in the design of their own living spaces. Since modern urban dwellers had largely given that skill over to professionals, he found he needed to introduce a language of design that all could understand.

Patterns capture expert advice in an easily transferable format. The present author claims no invention of what you will find here. These bits of advice come from many sources, including the personal practice of the author, but also from the agile literature and discussions with practitioners. See the references for the most important sources. Patterns use a structured format of presentation in which a problem is presented in its context. The forces that affect the expert's choice of solution are included, as well as the solution followed by some commentary. The advice needs to be general enough that it can be applied widely, but not so general as to be abstract. Patterns tell you what to DO when faced with a problem in a context.

The **pattern form** used here is as follows:

Name

Context paragraph: Who the pattern is addressed to and when in the cycle it can be applied.

???

Problem paragraph: The key sentence is in *italics*. What problem does the pattern address.

Forces paragraphs: What do you need to consider in order to apply this pattern? The forces are in bulleted lists.

! ! !

Therefore, solution paragraph: Key (usually first) sentence is in *italics*. What to do to solve the problem in this context.

Commentary and consequences paragraphs.

For several of the most important patterns, such as **Onsite Customer**, we also show a diagram with some of the important connections to other patterns here. There is also a larger example of connections in the Clusters of Patterns of Agile Development chapter at the end.

These are written in the "you" form as if the author is speaking to the person named in the pattern's context sentence. "You" could be a customer, a developer, or a manager, depending on the pattern.

In any pattern and in any discussion, the first use (at least) of the name of a pattern will appear in bold face. See **Onsite Customer** just above.

Thumbnail descriptions of all the patterns appear at the end of the book.

Pattern languages do more than individual patterns. They are sets of patterns that are both synergistically related and generative of what they describe. No individual pattern can completely resolve all of its forces. Therefore, other patterns, at a smaller "scale" help to resolve the remaining forces.

What is Agility?

Agility can mean many things, of course. If you think beyond software development it can mean never getting stuck. It means working forward using quick feedback loops based on recent results. It means always delivering value. Agility in software development grew out of a meeting of a group of people (The Hillside Group) whose lasting contribution is the Agile Manifesto: http://agilemanifesto.org

We are uncovering better ways of developing
software by doing it and helping others do it.
Through this work we have come to value:

Individuals and interactions over processes and tools

Working software over comprehensive documentation

Customer collaboration over contract negotiation

Responding to change over following a plan

That is, while there is value in the items on
the right, we value the items on the left more.

One of the simple, but key, ideas of agile software development practice is to take good practices, combine them, and then push them to the limit. If iterations are good, then do a lot of short iterations. If stakeholder-developer conversations are good, then crank that up to the maximum. For this to make sense, of course, the practices need to be the ones that really move us forward, and they need to be synergistically reinforcing.

Since patterns represent actions, this set of patterns is based on the various common practices of agile software development. There is a high degree of interaction between the patterns as there is between the practices. This implies great synergy in agile practice. A deep consequence of this is that you must choose the practices carefully since they support one another. If you decide not to do some practice you will not only lose the benefits of that practice, but also the support it gives to the others that you do perform. This requires compensation from additional practices if the balance of tension is to be maintained. Otherwise everything can fall apart. For example, **Pair Programming** is an important pattern and an important agile practice. If you do it you get many benefits. But if you don't, you also lose the lower defect rate and the sharing of knowledge about your project among team members provided by pairing. You then need to compensate for this with some other practice, such as code walk-throughs.

Some Key Ideas Explained

A few terms are used here in a technical sense that also have more general usage. This brief introduction will set the stage for their frequent appearance throughout the book.

Customer (Product Owner) In XP, Customer is a role and the term differs from common usage. He or she is that person entrusted by the organization to make all decisions about features of an application. It is a difficult role, sitting between the stakeholders and the developers. The intention is to give both parties a single point for resolving issues, so as to prevent chaos in the development process. In Scrum, the role is similar and is called the Product Owner.

Story: A short and simple description of a feature of an application. Stories are written on index cards (by the Customer) and indicate that a specification will later be gathered. Stories are estimated (by developers) in "points" to indicate the relative development difficulty. The set of stories for a project is called the Product Backlog.

Velocity: How many story estimation "points" a team is able to build successfully in one iteration.

Iteration/Sprint: A strictly time-boxed segment of a project. Usually one week to one month, but constant over any given project. The stories to be built in a sprint are the Sprint Backlog.

Release: An end-to-end subset of the functionality of a project that is robust enough to put into real usage. It is the product of one or more iterations.

Unit Test. A developer defined executable test for the feature under development. All unit tests are always passing, and are written before the feature is developed.

Acceptance Test. A Customer defined executable test that, when passing, assures that the application matches requirements.

Done. A feature is *done* when it will not need to be addressed further in the project. As a minimum it means coded, tested, documented, integrated into the application, optimized as necessary, and accepted by the Customer. When it is done, it can be deployed.

Refactor. The practice of improving the structure of code without changing its behavior. Practiced frequently to ease incorporation of new features into a product.

Scrum: A set of practices focusing on the overall running of a project. It focuses more on management than engineering and more on month-to-month rather than day-to-day activities. The key practices, as represented by patterns here, along with some of the pattern relationships, can be seen in the following diagram. Scrum is also the name given to the short daily meeting of the team within a Scrum project.

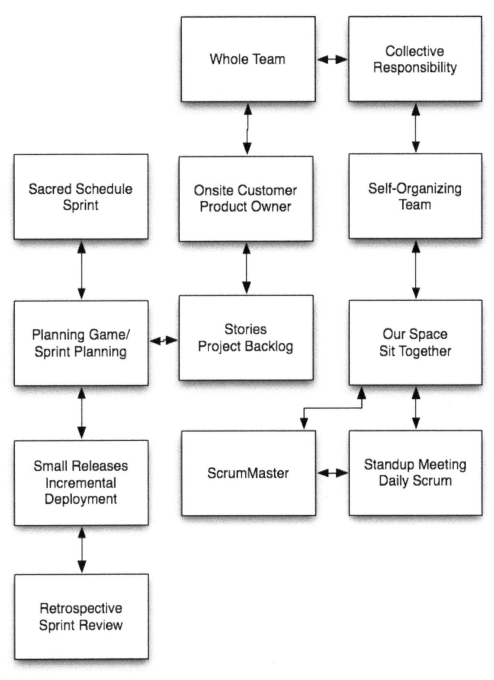

Scrum Patterns

Pigs and Chickens: Scrum has the notion of Pigs and Chickens [20]. The pigs are committed to the success of the project and careers will be affected by success or failure. Chickens are involved in the project, perhaps as users of the final project, or even funders, but their involvement is more remote. Only the pigs drive the project forward, and so only the pigs have a say in the process of the **Self Managing Team**. The chickens may only observe.

Extreme Programming (XP): A set of practices focusing on the day-to-day activities of a team. It is often used within Scrum, though the two are independent. The key practices, as represented by the patterns, along with some of the relationships can, be seen in the following diagram.

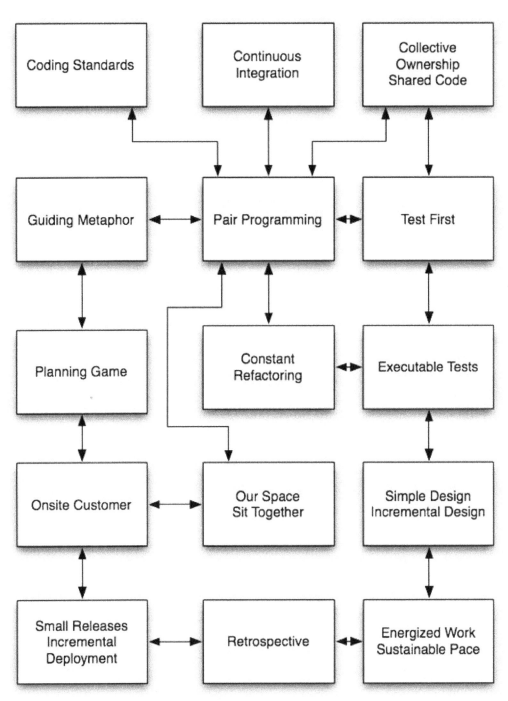

Extreme Programming Patterns

A Few Abbreviations

> XP is *Extreme Programming*
> ASD is *Agile Software Development*
> DTSTTCPW is *Do the simplest thing that could possibly work*, a pattern here
> YAGNI is *You ain't gonna need it,* a pattern here

An Agile Development Story (a.k.a. Fairy Tale)

A team has been formed by a **Sheltering Manager**, consisting of an **Onsite Customer**, seven developers, and a tech gofer with knowledge of infrastructure and tools issues that are customary in the organization. The **Whole Team** has found a workspace (**Our Space**) and set it up, both physically with tables for the workstations, and virtually with the development platform. The latter includes testing, code repository, and integration tools. The Whole Team along with the Sheltering Manager has gotten together for 3 days to **Train Everyone** under the direction of the **Effective Coach**. The Onsite Customer and the developers have gone through the initial development of the **Guiding Metaphor** and started on the **Planning Game**. The metaphor gives them an initial vocabulary to ease the communication between the customer and the developers.

The Sheltering Manager agrees to **Be Human**, and the Whole Team commits to the practices. While they know this will be difficult, they also trust the Manager to maintain a **Sustainable Pace** for the development. They have had some fun in the training sessions and those exercises have also helped to gel the team. The manager has assured everyone that they will be a **Self-Organizing Team.** This was reinforced by some of the training activities as well.

A day is spent with the Whole Team beginning the just-in-time requirements gathering. Thirty stories have been written, covering an **End To End** first cut at the desired functionality and the most important of these stories have been estimated by the team. The team has (Flexibly) set its **Initial Velocity** quite low as they are new to this project. A few of the stories were larger than can be accomplished in a single two-week iteration by an individual, so these have been broken into tasks and the **Implementer Estimates** these **Tasks**.

The customer chooses a few of the most important stories, looking at their value and their cost as reflected in the estimates. Development begins on just these stories, using **Test First** development with **Executable Tests**. Many questions are asked of the Onsite Customer and the answers to the **Questions Generate Acceptance Tests**. One of the developers works with the Onsite Customer to begin to develop an **Acceptance Test** suite for the application. Meanwhile, the developers **Program Promiscuously**, frequently changing partners so all are familiar with the code being developed. As each task is completed it is (**Continuously) Integrated** into the build, so that all unit tests pass. Of course all programmers **DTSTTCPW** in all coding and design, thereby **Delivering Value** to the customer. The **Onsite Customer Checks Off the Tasks** when they are done, reviewing unit tests as appropriate and noting the changes in the Acceptance Tests written and passing. Halts are called when Acceptance Tests that were passing suddenly fail. This is obvious since we use only Executable Tests and the suite is executed frequently; especially at each integration: several times each day.

The team holds daily **Standup Meetings** to flag difficulties and assure that each person knows what progress they will make that day. The Coach and **Social Tracker** keep the meeting going using advice from the Coach (ScrumMaster) on process, and the Tracker on progress. They hold the **Schedule Sacred** and will end the iteration at noon on Friday. The afternoon is used for **Retrospectives**, games, and the Planning Game for the next iteration.

The Coach works with the Onsite Customer to make sure that the first release (after one month) is both **End to End** and delivers **High Value First**. The Customer works with her own business groups to determine value and current required direction. She then uses this knowledge to guide the team via the Planning Game for each iteration. She continues to write stories and feeds them in to the process at iteration points to keep the direction consistent with her needs.

It takes the team a while to learn how to estimate effectively, and this becomes an issue at the Retrospective held at the end of each iteration. The Coach helps with suggestions and training games to make estimation more effective. The notion of **Personal Velocity** is initially foreign, but the Coach and Tracker get the developers to record their work in their **Project Diary** to give a baseline for their personal practice. After a couple of months the Coach makes only periodic visits to the team, but is on site for Retrospectives and is available to be called whenever the tracker or manager thinks it would be helpful.

The developers **Spike** when they must to learn how to estimate and build things. They **Refactor** the code whenever new stories can be built more easily by changing the existing code (improving its design). This is made easier as they own the code collectively and have been pairing promiscuously throughout. Thus they take **Collective Responsibility** for the project and its code. The Executable Tests give them the confidence that they don't break anything when they refactor.

They give **Full Communication** to the customer on opportunities, costs, and options available. As time permits they **Re-Estimate** a few of the older stories to keep the Planning Game short and sweet. They learn to give **Best Effort** at all times and to **Ask For More** when they complete tasks early. Conversely, the customer doesn't beat them up when they must **Gracefully Retreat** in an iteration when difficulties occur or unfortunately low estimates are occasionally made. The Customer learns that **Easy Does It** is a better policy than pushing (too) hard, though everyone demonstrates commitment and the nature of the work room makes everyone's effort obvious to all.

The Coach and Tracker, especially, manage the **Informative Workspace**, keeping everything visible, so that all stakeholders can see the current direction and measure the rate of progress toward the (ever changing) goal. **Cards and Whiteboards** are in evidence in the team space containing most of this information. Stakeholders with an interest in the project may attend the daily meetings without participating (as "chickens") and can see the progress in the **Informative Workspace**.

Alas, user level documentation was neglected for the early iterations, so a documentation specialist joins the (Whole) Team and starts to build the documentation structure that is henceforth kept up with the software development. Thereafter, **Documentation becomes Just Another Task**.

After several iterations and a few releases, the customer realizes that she now anticipates more work than the team can produce in the scheduled time available. She works with her business partners to choose between (a) later delivery of greater functionality, (b) earlier delivery of a smaller application, or (c) higher cost per week by growing the team methodically. She chooses the last option (after cost-benefit analysis) and the team decides to add two developers each iteration for the next two iterations. Pairing gives them the confidence that this won't slow them down by much and that the newbies will meld quickly into the team.

The project completes at the desired date. Some functionality that was thought desirable was not built, but the customer gives this low value. The overall cost is about 80% of the back-of-the-envelop estimate initially given for the project by executive management. The customer gets a promotion from her team. The developers hold a party to celebrate their raises, swearing fealty to the manager. They all live happily ever after.

Fundamental Patterns of Agility

There are a large number of practices and considerations that make agility possible and projects successful.

Sheltering Manager

You are a manager who is responsible for an agile project. The organization of which you are part may have little experience so far with this methodology.

???

Many things can disrupt any project, but when trying a new methodology one of the most difficult things for the team is when the rest of the organization is not on board. *When unnecessary disruptive influences impinge on the team they won't be able to concentrate on the task at hand.*

• Any new methodology is revolutionary in an organization. It will have supporters, skeptics, and detractors.

• Before you can judge the worth of a new methodology you need to give it a fair trial.

• To shelter a team requires either institutional power and prestige or great bravery.

• If the first agile project goes off the rails, the manager may be at risk.

• The team needs a safe environment in which to learn to change its practices.

! ! !

Therefore, *the manager's chief task is to shelter the team from disruptive influences of the rest of the organization.* Provide them with sufficient resources and keep the wolves at bay.

The Sheltering Manager can be the immediate supervisor or someone more remote. If the team comes from diverse parts of the organization it may need to be a high level supervisor or an especially cooperative team of lower level supervisors. Your job as the sheltering manager is to take the heat, but provide the light. In Scrum [20], those not committed to the project are kept away from the team and not permitted to influence it.

• You may become the focus of some sniping by detractors. You need to be prepared for this. Try not to let it reach the team, however.

• The team will largely manage itself, however. This will be a good thing if it works. Keep your eyes open for running off the rails, of course, but let **Self-Organizing Team** happen. Make sure they know they have the responsibility to do this and provide them the resources to make it possible.

• If you are not, yourself, knowledgeable about ASD include yourself when you **Train Everyone**. You need to know what to expect.

• Once your organization gains experience, however, you still need to remove obstacles from the path of the team.

See Patron Role in [5]. This pattern details an additional task for the Patron.

This pattern is connected to many others. The following diagram details some of the connections:

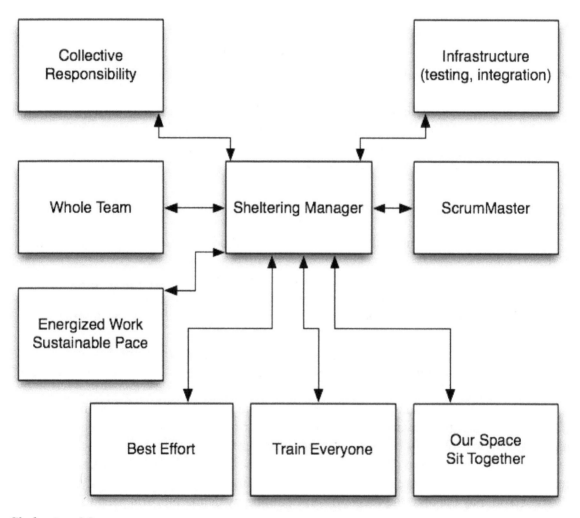

Sheltering Manager

Effective Coach

You are managing an Agile team, setting up the environment for success. Or you have been designated coach of an XP team, or ScrumMaster of a Scrum team.

???

No process can work if you don't perform its practices. Agile development requires more discipline than you might expect. This is especially true as some of the practices are counter-intuitive to many programmers. Many practices that are counter-productive in practice are ingrained in many work environments. People do these things "naturally" even though they know that they don't work.

• You want to give agile development a fair trial to see if it will work for you, but your habits are not aligned with the practices.
• The practices require discipline.
• Developers often don't want to consistently do all the practices.
• It can be difficult to know when something goes wrong how it might have gone better if the practices had been different.
• Not every practice is "right" in every circumstance. It takes experience to judge this.
• Everyone has a lot to do.

! ! !

Therefore, *someone on the team will have a full time role as Coach. The coach keeps the team faithful to the practices*. The coach role becomes part time after you have experience. Initially it will be helpful to have an external coach. Coaching is only one role of the ScrumMaster, however, but an important one.

• An external coach is expensive. A dedicated internal person is also expensive, perhaps even more so.
• Coaching is a role, not a job description. It can be shared and rotated in an experienced team. An external coach can train her successors. But budget enough so that the coaching is pervasive initially.
• The trainer can segue into a coach if you have someone with the right skills. The best coach is someone who has worked with several agile teams.
• Coaching costs money whether the coach is a regular employee or a hired consultant.
• A ScrumMaster, unlike a coach, needs some management authority, not over the team, but enough to push obstacles out of the way of the team. An external coach may not have the clout to do this effectively, in which case the **Sheltering Manager** must do it.

For your first agile project you are strongly encouraged to hire an external coach (or ScrumMaster) who is experienced with the practices. Gradually, the coaching function can be taken over by a team member. The coach is not a manager. It is her job to point out the consequences of not performing the practices, seeing when the practices are not working, and adapting the practices to the local situation. The coach needs to be present for at least the planning game sessions and the daily meetings. And of course, the coach needs to be experienced with XP, Scrum, and other agile techniques.

Note: Guard against the coach taking on a management function. A manager should not coach. Management should not ask the coach for member evaluations. The coach has a professional counseling role with the team.

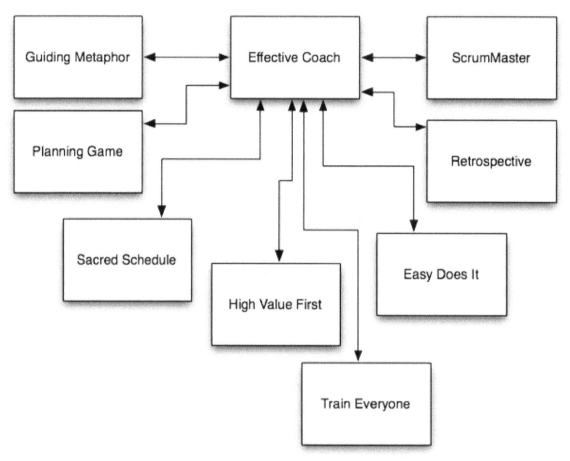

Effective Coach

ScrumMaster

You are setting up an agile team. You need to define roles of various individuals and assign them.

???

The job of being the customer or developer is hard enough without being continuously attentive to the process.

• Until the practices become second-nature to the team, they will fall back on other practices that may be counterproductive. This will be especially true when things get hard.

• Agile development requires not only knowledge and skill, but also process discipline.

• Many common practices in software development today are dysfunctional.

• Teams often find obstacles that hinder productivity. This might be needed resources or there might be sniping from outside the team, even from stakeholders.

! ! !

Therefore, *make someone responsible for the process itself.* An **Effective Coach** can fulfill part of this role, especially if there is also a **Sheltering Manager**.

• The ScrumMaster is not the manager. People don't work for the ScrumMaster. In particular, the daily **Stand Up Meeting** is not a report to the ScrumMaster. But he or she does advise the team on practice.

Technically the ScrumMaster (in Scrum Development) is responsible for process, but also responsible for clearing obstacles for the team. This implies some institutional knowledge and power, though there are people who can do this as external consultants.

When the **Stand Up Meeting** (Daily Scrum) identifies an obstacle to progress, the ScrumMaster is tasked with removing it. Alternatively the Effective Coach works with the Sheltering Manager to do so.

Note that there is some overlap between the roles of Sheltering Manager, Effective Coach, and ScrumMaster. Every team needs a Sheltering Manager and at least one of the others, but the roles are not interchangeable. A coach is not part of management and is often part of the team. The role can move from person to person in an experienced team. But in the absence of a ScrumMaster, the coach becomes responsible for the process and the manager for removing obstacles. When there is a ScrumMaster, he or she is not part of the team, but stands between the team and management. The ScrumMaster may or may not have a training and coaching role, beyond responsibility for process. The manager must always shelter, which often means removing obstacles, but is not responsible for process (Self Organizing Team), nor for coaching.

Onsite Customer (Product Owner)

You are the customer on an agile project. Development is progressing, or perhaps has just begun.

???

Without comprehensive requirements documentation, the agile developers need a source of "just in time" requirements.

• Agile projects don't develop all requirements at the beginning. These are gathered just in time to support their development.

• The developers need a pipeline to the stakeholders to get their questions answered as they arise. There will be a lot of questions since there are no comprehensive requirements documents.

• The developers need to work efficiently and not be cast into turmoil by hearing conflicting demands from the, possibly many, stakeholders.

• Any communication distance between the you and the developers will lead to increased cost and the wrong thing being built.

• Developers will make unfortunate assumptions when their progress is blocked for lack of information. This is unfortunate, but too true.

• The developers should make no business decisions at all. They have no control over what is to be built.

! ! !

Therefore, *stay immediately available to the team to develop stories and* **Acceptance Tests***, and to answer the many questions that the developers will have.* XP describes the customer as being continuously onsite with the rest of the team: working in the same room.

• The customer role is very demanding. It is easily the most demanding agile role.

• The developers have a source for answers, but you will find it difficult to do much else than serve the team. You may need a support staff to help with this job [16].

• In particular, the team will depend on you for executable Acceptance Tests and you may need help in creating these (**Customer-Tester Pair**).

• You are the sole determiner of what will be built in the project, and when it will be built, but of course, you must interact with the rest of the stakeholders to determine this.

• Your job is made harder so that the developers never have to slow down while disagreements play out.

• You need to be empowered by your organization to make all of the business decisions for the project: budget, features, business value, etc.

• Choosing the right customer can be a difficult task. The person chosen may need training in the task.

The customer takes a lead role in the **Planning Game**, developing **Stories**, and choosing those of high value for the next iteration and the next release. The product backlog needs to be kept in approximate value order. You can re-prioritize this at any time that you have new information.

It is useful to think of agile development as two funnels joined at the narrow ends. The stakeholders sit on one side and the developers on the other with the customer at the narrow part. All communication between developers and stakeholders is filtered through the customer.

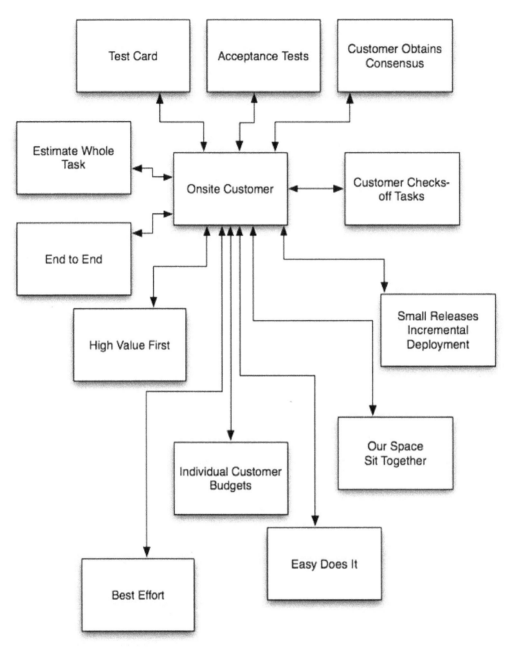

Onsite Customer

Whole Team

You are forming an agile team. It is time to decide the membership of the team.

???

Development requires several skills. While ASD pushes people to be generalists rather than specialists, specialized knowledge is often necessary, especially for a new team. Your project will fail if you don't have the needed skills available. *You need to assure that the needed skills can be brought to bear rapidly if you are to effectively respond to change.*

- Iterations are short and the team focuses on only the current **Stories**.
- Agile development depends on rapid communication turn-around.
- It is a highly collaborative process.
- When things get tough, people commit to their main task primarily.
- When a team needs to consult outsiders, it depends on the schedule and good will of those over which it has little influence.

! ! !

Therefore, *include everyone on the team who has a skill essential for its success.*

The team includes the customer and several developers, of course, but it may also include one or more analysts, test specialists, deployment/infrastructure experts, designers, UI experts, documentation writers, etc.

- Team members can come and go depending on the current need for their skills. That is to say, a specific skill may be needed for only part of the project. Bring in a person with the skills and make them part of the Whole Team.
- On the other hand, ASD favors generalists over specialists. The other practices will generate skill transfer in the long run.
- If you don't include someone essential, but depend on his skills, you will come into conflict with his own priorities, which are different from those of the team.
- You want a reasonably sized team, of course. Don't overdo it.

Scrum has the notion of Pigs and Chickens. The pigs are committed to the project and the success of the project is critical to their own success. The chickens are merely interested in the outcome. The Whole Team contains all the pigs.

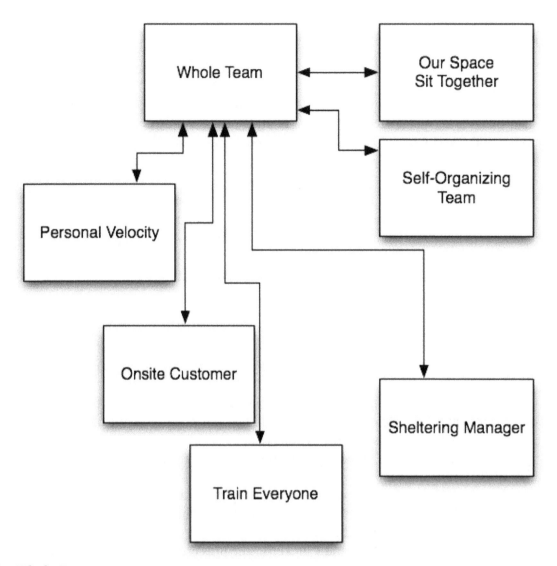

Whole Team

Train Everyone

You are someone who is initiating an agile project in an organization and you have a pretty good idea who the personnel will be. You might be a manager, or a change agent.

???

There are a lot of stakeholders in any project. There are a lot of skills needed to develop it. The **Whole Team** consists of everyone with an essential skill, including the customer who represents the business stakeholders. *Everyone has different ideas about how the project will proceed. If the methodology is new to the company, much of this information is faulty.*

• Team members may not have previously worked together.
• You are engaging in a project with a new methodology. No one is yet skilled in its use.
• Everyone will have a place in the development, but everyone needs to understand the role of everyone else.
• The team needs to work cooperatively and meld into a whole.
• Agile development requires a high level of discipline. Think of it as a highly choreographed dance.
• In ASD, most participants play a variety of roles.

! ! !

Therefore, *provide training that both shows everyone all the essential roles, but also brings the participants together as a team.*

Don't underestimate the importance of this. Select the team, including the customer. Bring in a trainer skilled in agile training and practice. Spend two or three days working together to introduce the required practices. The training should have an intellectual (reading/ listening/ discussing) component, but also an active component. Let people play roles in the training that are not their normal roles. Your goal in designing the training is not only to let people understand agile development at a deeper level, but also to begin to build an effective team.

• Training will cost you both time and money.
• You may need to return to training after the project runs for a while. Having a **Retrospective** at a release point can let you know if this is necessary.
• The trainer(s) can, perhaps, later stay on to coach. This is not essential, but you will likely need an external **Effective Coach** if this is a first agile project. The coach needs to know what training was done, in any case.

There are several available training programs. Some of them are quite fun. Some focus on a few practices of XP and some on the process as a whole. The team can be asked to create something other than software. This lets non-programmers act as developers and permits programmers to take the customer role. The goal of the training is twofold: (a) demonstrate the effect of not carrying out the practices, and (b) bring the team together as a cohesive unit.

Hint: Include management in the training, especially the **Sheltering Manager**. The author created an XP training exercise that covers all aspects of Extreme Programming in a day. It is accessible to managers, customers, and developers: Extreme Construction. See:

http://csis.pace.edu/~bergin/extremeconstruction/index.html

One Project

You are the **Sheltering Manager** for an agile team, deciding on how to allocate work to people.

???

In the face of uncertainty, you don't have a comprehensive plan for the entire project. You need a way to develop sound projections for the completion.

• It is common in organizations for people to work on more than one project at a time.

• The team velocity is your primary projection tool, but it needs to stabilize to be useful.

• If developers have another project to work on, then when they finish current tasks they will naturally devote additional time to the other project. Then velocity of this project can decrease, but not increase. They will never **Ask For More**, but they might need a **Graceful Retreat**. Projecting the team's work will become much more difficult.

• The knowledge of the project is in the heads of the team members, not in any comprehensive documentation. It is difficult to keep disparate things straight.

! ! !

Therefore, *the key developers on the project should be assigned only this one project.*

• Using **Yesterday's Weather** to set the next iteration velocity will never be valid if you don't have full commitment from the developers and you are left with pure guessing, since the requirements of the other project are likely variable and will cause intense pressure. In practice, a 60/40, say, split never works. This is especially true if the other projects are on behalf of different stakeholders

• Nor does it work to pull a developer off a team for an iteration or so. They take important information when they go and will need to learn it again if they return. See **Team Continuity** for more. If you really need a person elsewhere, use something like **Grow Up** before they leave so their knowledge stays with the team.

• If you have ten developers and need 60 percent of the time for this project, assign six of them to this project only and the others to the other work. If this is too hard, see **Rapid Response Teams**, but One Project is far better.

• If developers work on more than one project for different managers, then a hostile or skeptical manager of the other project can starve your project for developer time. This has been observed in the wild.

Self-Organizing Team

You are managing an agile team and want to organize it to maximize likelihood of success.

???

You want an effective team, but you are in a situation of high uncertainty or high flux. *You may think you understand what needs to be done, but you don't know as much as you think you do.*

• Taylorism applied to intellectual work seldom succeeds.
• The best decisions are seldom made by a single person.
• Telling people what to do is seldom a way to motivate them effectively.
• Individuals on a team want to succeed both individually and collectively.
• A management-directed team will lessen cooperation among team members as people will define "success" as pleasing you individually.
• People want to make a difference.
• Individuals are more likely to be personally invested in a project in which they have the opportunity to set the conditions.

! ! !

Therefore, l*et the team organize itself. Don't assign tasks and roles, or even processes.*

• The team that takes on its own organization takes on responsibility for success.
• The manager's task becomes one of clearing obstacles and enabling **Energized Work**.
• **Retrospectives** can help you keep on track.
• There must be **Collective Responsibility**. This also implies shared reward.

Scrum has the notion of "Pigs and Chickens." The chickens are involved in the project, but the pigs are committed [20]. While the chickens can offer advice, only the pigs can make decisions. But they need to be free to make those decisions without outside interference as long as they can continue to make good progress.

We note that modern militaries, usually thought of as the prototypical hierarchical organizations, seldom apply top-down control at the sharp end of the stick. A US Marine squad is a Self-Organizing Team.

See Advice For Customers.

Note: http://en.wikipedia.org/wiki/Frederick_Winslow_Taylor is the father of Taylorism.

Just Start

You are organizing a new project, perhaps taking a manager role or technical lead. You are spending a lot of time trying to get started on the first project.

???

Sometimes the organization can take forever in trying to make decisions on how to start a new project with a new methodology. Everyone needs to understand how it will work. Everyone seems to want to wait until all questions are answered.

• Many teams starting agile are still stuck in the mode of trying to gather all requirements before you begin.

• There may be fear of failure among many participants.

• Working software is the best proof of any new methodology.

• Agile processes can be tuned as you go, both the direction of the project itself, and the practices of the team and the stakeholders. Nothing needs to be decided only once in an agile project.

• It is hard to make big and expensive errors in an agile project, other than ignoring what you know must be true.

! ! !

Therefore, *just start the project and let everyone learn through the first couple of iterations how it works and what its tradeoffs are.* If you learn it was a mistake, you won't have spent a lot of time and money.

• This can be risky, and someone needs to put up some initial funding to make this happen. A **Nano-Project** might be a safer way to begin.

• Make sure you have an **Effective Coach** or **ScrumMaster** to guide these initial iterations so that the practices are learned and the stakeholders can get more comfortable with the process.

The author worked on a project that spent months in discussion, followed by a nearly equal project phase. The team could have been finished in half the time, or delivered twice what they did. Nothing important was actually decided or changed in this initial discussion period. Finally they realized that if they didn't Just Start they would never end.

Guiding Metaphor (Topos)

You are a member of an agile team. The project is just beginning. You want to understand in general terms what the application is about.

???

Customer and developers often fail to have a shared view of the project. They speak different languages and live in different worlds.

• Customers and developers have different training, backgrounds, terminology, and even world-views.

• Developers are often influenced by what they built in some previous project.

• Customers often assume that everyone's concerns are the same as theirs. Much of their view of the world is implicit: business value, business process, etc.

• It is difficult to build something without an overall view, but agile projects may not create an overall design at the beginning.

• People are good at learning from metaphor and analogy.

! ! !

Therefore, *spend enough **Face Time** developing a common, shared, story about the application.* It should have sufficient detail that it gives a coherent picture of the system that can be shared by the stakeholders and the developers.

• The Guiding Metaphor is not a specification. "Just enough" is enough.

• The metaphor should be able to tell you when you have gone wrong, though not the precise direction. It is intended to give you overall guidance only.

• The metaphor will need to evolve with the project, of course. If you change direction radically, the current Guiding Metaphor may become obsolete.

• This is most needed when the **Onsite Customer** and developers are working together for the first time.

• Someone on the stakeholder side likely has a grand view; the "grand unified theory," of the product to be created. Have him or her try to express this to the developers. Often this stakeholder is very passionate and enthusiastic about this view. Express that.

• An **Effective Coach** may help the team recognize whether or not the view is shared.

At the beginning of an agile project, the target may be seen only indistinctly. This is expected. But the customer has some idea of where she needs to get over the life of the project. It is necessary to share this view with the developers in a way that can guide their thinking as they go. Sometimes role-playing games are a good way to communicate the basic structure of the customer's goal.

In many ways, this is the hardest of the XP practices. So hard, in fact, that some have dropped it. However, projects can fail without a shared vision of the target. One of the difficulties is that customers are not trained to communicate their vision to those who don't share it and who don't necessarily understand their needs, goals, and constraints. Customers (and stakeholders in general), need an "elevator talk" with which they can explain the project to a stranger in two minutes or less.

28

Best Effort

You are a member of an agile team and are trying to define the basic relationship between all of the parties. You might be the manager. Say, you are using XP in a project for which it is appropriate; the requirements are either not known in advance or it is known that they will change during the project.

???

Management and people paying bills like to have contracts for delivery of software. Since software is a creative human endeavor it is rarely possible to be successful with this approach, especially if the requirements can't be nailed down at the start. Agile teams do not try to capture all requirements prior to beginning development, so the target of the project is not clearly and completely defined at the beginning. The customer remains involved to steer the project to a fairly fine level of detail and the team will give feedback continuously on costs and risks. The essence of agility is that the team can react to changing conditions at reasonable cost.

• People often take estimates as a contract. They sometimes insist on it. However, if estimation is inherently inaccurate, then no one wins by insisting on delivery.

• The thing doesn't get built just because someone insists that it must.

• Something about the project is such that it is not possible to gather accurate and stable requirements at the beginning.

• Underestimates and overestimates can both waste resources.

• In some organizations it is common practice to hide information from one another.

• What you (as a manager) really need is a system of estimates that are useful for planning whether they are precise or not.

• Agile development tries hard to avoid blame. Blame doesn't move the project forward.

• Agile development has other, more effective, ways to decide when to stop paying for product.

! ! !

Therefore, *offer the contract of Best Effort and complete communication.* The customer will have complete information on which to base business decisions and can redirect or terminate the project at any time there is insufficient value delivered. Ideally termination is when good business value has been given and only low priority/high cost features remain.

• If you can know the requirements in advance and they will not change, agile development may not be not your best methodology.

• In agile development, you pay something for this flexibility to change requirements that you need not pay if they won't change. Agile development saves money by delaying expensive decisions and avoiding building low value features.

    • To achieve this, however, you must build **High Value** Stories **First**.

    • The tradeoff is that you get what you can for a reasonable effort and you don't need to guess what you may need in the future.

    Many projects try to over-specify a project. As Beck explains in [2] there are four variables: cost, features, schedule, and quality. You can only specify three of these and the fourth is dependent. Many projects try to specify all of them in a contract, but in reality the schedule slips and so becomes the dependent variable, or worse, everything slips. In agile development the features variable is explicitly made the dependent variable. Features may slip in an iteration, but the others are held fixed.

    The team's measured velocity over time, together with the measured granularity of the story estimates, make management projection of cost and time efficient and effective.

    Also see **Negotiated Scope Contract**.

This pattern also works on a smaller scale, when you are working within a single iteration. The developers, in the **Planning Game**, promise Best Effort to the Product Owner and the Product Owner accepts this as the only "contract."

Sprint

You are an agile team. You are deciding on how long to make an iteration.

???

You can get a lot done in a long iteration, but that adds risk.

• At the end of an iteration you get feedback that guides your way forward.

• Short iterations require a lot of work from the customer to write small stories and from the developers to break the bigger stories into tasks that can be done simultaneously.

• Long iterations let you do more, but it takes longer to know you are off the rails.

• Things change in the larger organization. In a six-month iteration, too much will likely have changed.

! ! !

Therefore, *iterations should be very short:* A week to a month. Iterations deliver business value as determined by the **Onsite Customer**. They are strictly time-boxed.

• You can go **Beyond Extreme** and do daily iterations. This depends on the granularity of the stories, of course.

• The more uncertainty you have about the project, the shorter the Sprint.

Two weeks is pretty typical in XP and one month is canonical in Scrum.

The term Sprint comes from Scrum.

Planning Game (Sprint Planning Meeting)

You are a member of an agile team. An iteration (sprint) is about to begin. You need to decide what to do in this iteration.

???

The customer needs a chance to look at recent events and current needs and to re-steer the project. If you continue on the wrong path for long, you will fail.

• You want to permit rapid re-targeting of the project. Business needs change.
• You don't want day-to-day flux to introduce chaos into the work.
• You want guidance from the customer, but not micromanagement.
• The stories have to get estimated
• The stories need to get selected for an iteration.
• If you fail to plan, you plan to fail. (Wisdom from "Planned Development" but no less relevant to agile development.

! ! !

Therefore, *set aside one day a month (perhaps distributed over shorter iterations) to plan the next iteration and/or release.*

• This should often include a **Retrospective** of the previous cycle.
• Within an iteration the work plan is fixed, though things known to have become obsolete are dropped. Work isn't added unless the team runs out of work.
• Developers will **Ask For More** if they find they have additional time.
• Arbitrary changes of direction are permitted (welcomed) at the planning game points.
• The Planning Game is held once per iteration, whatever the length.
• If release cycles are longer than iteration cycles, planning for release is also done in the Planning Game.

Scrum plays the Planning Game once a month, XP every week or two. In both it is a time-boxed activity, since you want to **Deliver Customer Value**. Since the interval is longer, the **ScrumMaster** might, on occasion, need to declare premature end to a sprint, especially when changes to business plans make current work foolish. This is less likely in XP with shorter iterations. In any case it is a rare occurrence. A new Planning Game will then begin a new cycle, perhaps after a Retrospective.

Stories (Product Backlog)

You are a member of an agile team, probably its **Onsite Customer**. You recognize that there is work that needs to be done. This could be a feature desired by a stakeholder, infrastructure work, or even coordination with other teams.

???

You need a simple way to communicate about the requirements, without actually completely specifying them long before development.

• In the absence of complete requirements, you need a prioritized *backlog* of work for the developers.

• Agile works by doing requirements gathering for one feature followed immediately by development of those requirements and testing that the requirement is satisfied. You don't need a long document to describe a feature.

• The customer is assumed to be present to answer questions that arise. Rather than capture the answers in documentation, capture them in code and tests.

• Your requirements are likely to change. So effort expended on requirements gathering may be discarded.

! ! !

Therefore, *describe the features and requirements in a sentence or two on index cards: one per feature.*

• Name the stories and use the names in communication. This works far better than merely numbering them. You may want the numbers for tracking, but the names need to be evocative of the intent of the requirement.

• The great majority of the stories are written by the **Product Owner** (Onsite Customer). The set of stories is called the Product Backlog and it is owned and prioritized by the Product Owner.

• The stories form the basis of the **Planning Game**. The estimates provided there are the key to agile estimation and planning.

• The stories are not requirements. Instead they are a notation that a requirement exists. Stories are initially understood well enough to estimate them. When a story shows up in an iteration (in the Sprint Backlog, that is), it is then completely understood. Thus, the requirements are gathered just-in-time in the form of executable tests. This too, lowers the cost of change.

One of the best and most informative things I ever heard about requirements is that they can be complete or consistent, but not both. Sufficiently complex systems always seem to have this character. If you do "just enough, just in time" you avoid this difficulty as well as give yourself the flexibility to change direction rapidly. The tests that you write as you go, keep your project consistent, or make it immediately clear when it isn't.

Note that the uncertainty about the role addressed here in the context paragraph comes from the fact that occasionally stories need to come from the developers themselves. This is to get needed infrastructure scheduled in the same way as other tasks. Such stories are also estimated and scheduled in the normal way so that velocity can be measured properly.

Initial Velocity

You are collectively the developers on an agile team. You are in the **Planning Game** of the first iteration.

???

You need to project what the team can accomplish in the first iteration, but you have no history on which to make the projection.

• Velocity is a measure of how much work can be done by a team (or individual) in a fixed amount of time. The estimates, however, are measured either in ideal time or simply in relative time. It is essentially impossible to give real-time estimates as they are too variable.

! ! !

Therefore*, the first iteration velocity is a small fraction of what the team believes can be done in the available developer time as measured in some convenient unit (often days).* A good rule of thumb is 30%.

• Some projects start with an initial velocity of 0 and just do as much work, as they can in the first iteration, with enough stories to keep everyone busy. It might be best to choose relatively simple stories that the customer agrees **Deliver Customer Value**. The down-side of this is that the developers can't do any optimization over a fixed body of work in that iteration.

• After the first iteration, just use **Yesterday's Weather** to set velocity.

• If the developers finish this work they will **Ask For More**.

Some projects never get far from a 30% ratio of velocity to real time. Some organizations hold a lot of meetings that are not optional. Also, on different projects, different kinds of difficulties occur. In this case a **Retrospective** can help you figure out how to do estimation better.

An "ideal programmer day" is a day in which the person can code for eight hours with no other concerns or interruptions. The phone never rings, the person is healthy and rested, etc. Few people ever actually work such a day. One way to give story estimates is in ideal programmer days. This is initially a difficult concept.

"Relative estimation" on the other hand, simply measure the "size" of a story relative to other stories done in the past. "We estimated that one as 4 and this one seems to be about as difficult and has similar characteristics, therefore this one should also be a 4." This method is initially impossible as you have no prior experience on this project to draw on.

It is usually a good idea to start with ideal programmer days and morph over time to simple **Relative Estimates.**

High Value First

You are a customer on an agile project and you are involved in the **Planning Game**. You are trying to decide which stories to schedule in the next few iterations or sprints.

???

Stories have different business value. They have different development costs. The effort to develop a product should be commensurate with its business value. *Development resources can be wasted on low value features.*

• In top-down (structured, waterfall) development the developers often don't get good guidance as to the relative business value of the features required. They may spend a lot of effort (time and money) on low value features. This should be avoided.

• From the customer's standpoint, some features are essential and some "would be nice to have." Often eighty percent of the business value is derived from 20% of the features.

• The customer needs to be able to assign value to each story she writes. The developers will assign it a cost (the estimate). This can be difficult.

• For most purposes a rough relative value between stories is all that is essential, at least at the beginning of a project.

• The value will change over time as business conditions and strategies change.

! ! !

Therefore, *build the high value, most essential, stories first. When the value curve and the cost curve cross, cancel the project.* And note that no scaffolding was put in place to support these low value features since you have always **DTSTTCPW**. At any point, schedule the highest value remaining stories in the next available iterations. If the cost of a story is higher than its value you can often split the story into its essential and inessential parts. Once these parts are re-estimated you may be in a better position to proceed.

• This assumes, of course, that your estimate of value is measurable and *accurate*. This is often difficult to achieve. However, the estimates don't need to be *precise*.

• Short iterations force you to think in terms of small granularity features. This makes estimation easier, but partitioning harder. If something important is more complex than can be done in an iteration it must be split. When this is fundamentally impossible ASD may not be an ideal approach.

• It also assumes that the value is more than the cost implied by the estimate provided by the developers.

• There is an additional cost here, since the developers don't see every story from the beginning, they cannot make certain optimizations that might lower cost.

• But these optimizations will waste money if requirements change and make them obsolete. Agile developers don't anticipate what might be true in the future.

• Complicating this is the fact that the first release needs to create an **End To End** version of the product. Some features will be omitted or be in skeleton form only.

The value of stories will then generally decrease as the project progresses. The cost will generally increase, as it gets harder to incorporate new stories as you go along. **Refactoring**, tries to keep this rising cost curve as flat as possible by keeping the design coherent even as new things are added. At some point, however, the remaining stories are probably not worth building. Note that this is one of the major ways that agile processes can save money over planned development: the low value requirements are just dropped. This may also deliver you a product sooner.

In extremely volatile situations the crossing curves effect may not occur. You might only learn of a high value requirement late in the process so the value curve might take a sharp upward turn. But this ability to quickly retarget the project toward a different goal delivers value in a different way: you get a more suitable product.

Deliver Customer Value

You are any member of an agile development team and are at a point at which several actions are possible in the near term.

???

You want everyone to win, but you are in a situation of high uncertainty or high flux. It can be difficult to decide whether to build infrastructure for the project or work toward getting the next feature done. *You want to enable rational decision making on the next steps to take.*

- Too many projects deliver plans and documents, but no working software.
- Some programmers like to build "cool" but speculative code, that is not directly related to the task at hand.
- Many projects are hard to track because they spend so much time at the beginning on scaffolding, much of which is eventually discarded. This is especially true when requirements change for whatever reason.

! ! !

Therefore, *choose the path that delivers best customer value now.*
- Customers will be happier and can better judge how to steer the project if they see tangible results.
- The customer steers, of course. The wise customer chooses **High Value First**.
- Speculation about what might be needed in the future will cost you in many ways if it is not needed. Remember that change is likely to occur, so don't over commit to infrastructure. Just enough. Just in time.
- Simple solutions deliver value now, without speculating about what "might be needed" in the future.
- "Just enough, just in time" is a good mantra for evaluating all of the subsidiary issues.
- Short iterations (**Sprint**) and **Small Releases** helps you here.

An implication of this is that a customer can cancel the project when she judges that sufficient value has been delivered and that the costs of continuing are more than the expected benefits. This is one major way in which agile development saves money.

However, deliver *real* value. Neglecting testing, documentation, or integration so that you can "deliver" a feature (even though it isn't "done") doesn't really deliver value.

Yesterday's Weather

You are a developer on an agile team. You are in the **Planning Game** for any iteration except the first. (If it is the first iteration see **Initial Velocity**).

???

*To plan the iteration, the **Onsite Customer** needs to know how much work she can expect to be completed so that she can select **Stories**.* Velocity is how many story points can be completed in an iteration.

• It is important for project planning that the velocity stabilize over time.

• The work can change over time. It may not be possible to spread out the "hard bits."

• Everyone develops a rhythm of work and thought. This means that new stories are likely to be similar to recent ones.

! ! !

Therefore, *the velocity for the next iteration is the number of story points completed and accepted by the customer in the previous one.*

• The first iteration is different, of course. See **Initial Velocity**.

• It is a simple matter to adjust proportionately if people are ill or go on vacation.

• If a team has just added a member, don't make a proportional adjustment. Just **Ask For More** if you complete early with the new member.

• Don't give a larger velocity hoping to please the customer. Adding work later is much less disruptive to the process than dropping work. We value completed and accepted stories and nothing less.

• A story is "done" when we no longer need to address anything about it. This means not only coded, but documented, tested, integrated into the application, and accepted by the customer with all tests passing. Only then do we count it as part of the velocity for this iteration.

Test First

You are a developer in the development phase of a project. You are beginning programming; perhaps the development of a task or subtask, or perhaps refactoring or bug fixing. You are pretty confident you know what to do for a task, though you may not yet be sure how to do it.

???

You think differently when writing tests than when writing code. Testing requires that you take a broader view. Coding requires a microscopic view. *Tests written after a task is coded too often test what was done, not what is wanted, if they get written at all.*

• Testing takes time. But debugging takes more time and is more frustrating.
• In an agile project things will change. Changes in future may invalidate assumptions you make now. You need to make these assumptions visible.
• You want to build what the story says to build, but ONLY that. You want to **DTSTTCPW**.
• You feel some pressure, of course, to "just get on with it."
• Programming is creative work. It requires thinking as well as coding.
• You can design while testing. You can test while designing.
• You need to assure your tests capture your intent, not just your implementation.

! ! !

Therefore, *write your tests for some code before you write the code*. If the tests pass you are done. Capture your understanding in the test. Write no code without a failing test. This is also known as Test Driven Development (TDD). These developer-defined tests are called *unit tests*.

• If your organization has a testing group that will develop its own tests from some requirements documents (here just story cards) then this can seem like wasted effort. If you can get a member of the test group on your team, you will probably be able to write better tests and you might be able to feed your tests into their process. In other words, your tests might help them. But their traditional tests, coming late, won't help you.

• The purpose of unit tests is not the same as that of **Acceptance Tests**. Unit tests test that you build what you think you should build. Acceptance Tests test what the customer wants built: what you actually should build. You need both. The customer writes or specifies the Acceptance Tests. The developer creates the unit tests.

• It will take the team time and effort to get comfortable with this practice. It also requires initial setup before the project begins. The coach can help with the former.

• Note that you work in very short test-implement cycles. Write a single test. Make it pass. Repeat. Don't try to write a lot of tests and then make them all pass at once. You will tend to forget where you are and get confused. The cycle is like the beating of your heart. The cycle ends when you can't think of anything else that could go wrong. Of course you do boundary tests, stress tests, etc. as you would normally do if you were a professional tester.

• Write only enough code to make the test pass. Then think again about what other tests are needed. This saves you money, since you are less likely to build bloat into the application by programming speculatively.

There are three ways to fail when you write tests after the code.

(a) Time constraints will push you away from writing the tests.

(b) You will be tempted to get too creative when programming, thinking that some extension could be easily added. So why not? If what you do isn't needed, it is a waste of the customer's resources, complicates the code, and needs to be maintained in future.

(c) You will spend time in the coding process doing design without capturing your decisions in tests. You aren't saving time, as the thinking process uses the bulk of your time in any case.

Unit tests have all of the benefits of any regression test system. **Executable Tests** give you confidence that you got it right the first time, but more importantly, they let you **Refactor** with confidence. They also tell you immediately that a new requirement is inconsistent with an old one.

Anecdote: The author once sat down to build a feature in a project, wrote a test for the feature, and it passed without any additional code for the feature. In fact the feature was implemented as an unintended side effect of other features. Don't count on this happening often, though.

Special note on testing: This author believes (with only anecdotal evidence) that when correctly done, testing doesn't cost you time, but speeds you up. This implies that you are using **Pair Programming** and test driven development *and* you are doing your thinking, designing, and planning for a story while strapped into the test harness. You must think about the structure of your solution. You must design classes and methods to solve the problem. If you do this planning and thinking with JUnit (or equivalent) running you will capture all of your decisions immediately as tests. The planning needs to be done anyway. The tests serve then as notes about your decisions as well as the tests that will eventually prove your code. While this may not be true for tests of GUI code, it seems to be for tests of the underlying model. This is another reason for clean separation between model and view, actually.

Executable Tests

You are a member of an agile team. You must develop effective unit and Acceptance Tests.

???

Tests must be run often so that the project doesn't veer off into the woods. Manual testing is expensive and tedious.

• Both the developers and the customers depend on tests to know where they are, since you don't have comprehensive requirements documentation for this.

• In an iterative project that is using test driven development, the tests are exercised frequently. This gives you assurance that you haven't broken something.

• At every change or addition to the code base, the tests need to be re-run to be sure that a change hasn't broken something or invalidated earlier assumptions. See **Continuous Integration**.

• Manual testing is tedious. So tedious that most people will ignore it and hope for the best. Manual tests are hard to execute and therefore are not run often. This can lead to too much development between runs of the test suite and then many problems making the tests run and fixing the bugs.

• You need to be able to test at different levels of granularity. You should be able to test a single class, a single story, or the entire state of the application. This requires good tools and good test design.

• There are a lot of tests.

• Some things the customer wants to specify are very difficult to specify in an executable way. But when done, the customer has confidence in the result.

! ! !

Therefore, *capture tests in a way in which they can be directly executed*. Unit tests can use something like JUnit. **Acceptance Tests** can use something like FIT/FitNesse. The tests should be collected into suites that can be run all together. Tests are the primary measure of progress.

• You need to be able to run all tests at every code commit point. You need to have a policy about what happens when some test fails at a commit point. In some projects everything else halts until the tests pass. This practice is considered normal, not extreme, in XP.

• You need tools and frameworks for executable tests, especially for user interface tests. You need machine cycles for their execution. See **Ten Minute Build**.

• Start to get your test framework in place prior to your first iteration. If you use any special technology, then investigate specialized testing tools you may need whenever it becomes necessary. Don't underestimate the difficulty of finding and learning the right test framework for your particular tools and technology. Many of them are free, but have little support. Many can be found on Sourceforge (http://sourceforge.net).

 • While it is possible to use robot driven test tools to test GUI parts of the application, these often take a long time to execute and may require user intervention. This gives additional incentive to make clean design breaks between model and view, so that the underlying business logic is all in the model and can be effectively tested independent of its interface. Then the GUI tests test focus on the look of the interface, rather than its behavior. End-to-end testing is still necessary, of course.

 • The customer will need help in making Acceptance Tests automatic. Make this a task [16]. Helping the customer formulate the Acceptance Tests is a role.

 The **Effective Coach** can encourage the team so that tests are written. The **Social Tracker** can track and plot the number of tests and the number of passing Acceptance Tests using **Information Radiators**. The shape of these curves can tell you when you are starting to slow down development. This can imply that costs are rising, that stories are getting harder to build, and especially that it is time for serious **Refactoring**.

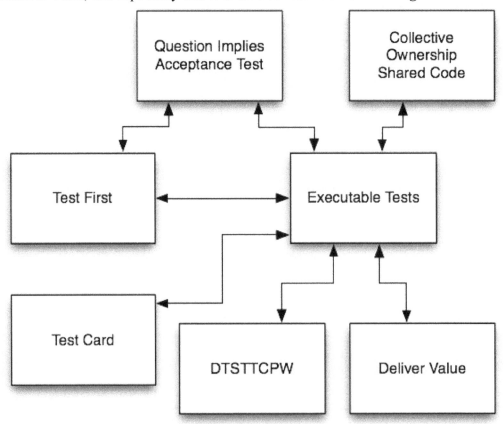

Executable Tests

Collective Responsibility

You are the overall manager of an agile team. You need to set expectations of rights and responsibilities for those who work on the team.

???

Agile Development is a lot about rights and responsibilities. It is also a lot about sharing information and skill building. *You need a high performance team in which every individual is deeply committed to every aspect of success of the project.*

• Individual responsibility is best for assigning blame when things go wrong, but not for reinforcing cooperation.

• When responsibility is individual it is often possible to know why something failed and to assign blame: Some individual didn't fulfill some task.

• However, this doesn't aid cooperation in a team. In extreme cases people believe that their only security is what they know that others on the team don't know, making development into a zero-sum game.

• If responsibility is shared and things go wrong you either need to blame everyone or no one at all. But blame doesn't build software.

! ! !

Therefore, *give the responsibility for completion and for the artifacts to the team itself, not to individuals*. Let the team itself manage the fine-grained aspects of this.

• A consequence of this is that the reward structure must also be collective. It should not be possible for an individual to succeed while the team fails, nor for an individual to fail while the team succeeds, except in extraordinary circumstances.

• Agile development tries hard to avoid blame. When problems arise, give them to the team to solve. **Effective Coaches** and **ScrumMasters** can help with finding ways out of problem areas, particularly if the problem is due to lack of discipline in following the agreed practices. The short iteration cycles here help you, as problems are likely to be noticed earlier and, as a consequence likely to be of smaller scale than otherwise. Solving problems can help build the team, in fact.

• On the other hand, an agile team exerts quite a lot of pressure on its own members. The pressure can be positive or negative. In the best situations, the pressure to conform to team norms will tend to bring an errant member back into the fold. A coach needs to watch that the pressure stays positive. It is fine to not want to let the team down. It isn't good if someone is the goat. Some teams assign all blame to an imaginary team member or even to a member who agrees to always take the blame. Blame Chet [12].

• If you have a completely introverted hero hacker, don't normally put her on an agile team.

Note: There are certain situations in which Collective Responsibility is not possible.

For example, in safety critical software you may have certain arcane skills known to only a small number of the developers. While it is preferable, in general, to spread these skills, it may not be possible. These may not be good candidates for ASD practice, of course, or may require partitioning of the project or additional practices to compensate for the needs.

Note that **Constant Refactoring**, in particular, won't work without Collective Responsibility as that practice implies that anyone that sees the need to change code can do so. **Pair Programming** and **Collective Code Ownership** reinforce it.

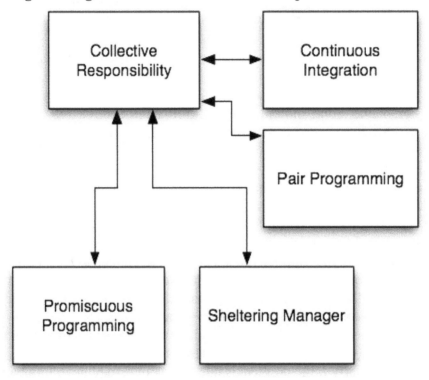

Collective Responsibility

Stand Up Meeting (Daily Scrum)

You are an agile team. It is 8am on any day of the development phase.

???

Software development works best when everyone knows what is going on. New information comes to the customer and to the developers constantly. Some of this knowledge affects what others must do, but the person receiving the information may not know the consequences that it implies for others on the team.

• Long meetings waste everyone's time and are often boring for most participants.

• You need to know where you are and where you are headed in the short term in an agile team. In particular, you may need to know what others are working on for effective refactoring.

• Changes in the business may make some things especially important or unimportant in the short term.

• What one person on an agile team knows, others should know as well.

• You don't need to solve every problem as a team.

• A potential danger of frequent meetings (even short ones) is that the customer will try to over-steer the project.

! ! !

Therefore, *hold a 15 minute stand-up meeting every day*. No one sits unless they have a physical need. If you don't stand up, the meeting will last too long. The customer is present as well as the rest of the team. Only those with a stake in the project get to participate: In Scrum terminology, the pigs can talk, but not the chickens. In Scrum, this meeting is called the Scrum.

The **Social Tracker** is an important part of the meeting. He or she gives a quick report. If there are problems then say where. The meeting is led by the tracker, the ScrumMaster, or the coach rather than by the customer or management.

• Short meetings can bring everyone up to speed and let everyone know the current level of risk. It is not a report to management or to the customer, but intended to inform the members of the team.

• Issues are not solved at this meeting, though individuals may be assigned to solve them. The **Effective Coach** can keep the meeting moving. Everyone says what they are working on at the moment and if there are any problems on the horizon that they see. In Scrum [20] the rule is: say what you worked on yesterday, say what you will work on today, say what obstacles you see to your success.

• One possible danger of the stand up meetings is that some customers will try to use them to micro-steer the build. The Effective Coach can help guard against this. The customer changes direction only at the **Planning Game** points. The customer may, of course, drop work from an iteration as soon as it is known that changing conditions have made it obsolete. New work may then, perhaps, be able to be added when the team finishes the rest of the work in the iteration and has more time available (**Ask For More**). The customer doesn't add or change work in an iteration and cannot look on the stand-up as an opportunity to do so.

   • Don't let the short meeting get long. It should be at the same time every day. If everyone is present early have it then. If not, then it is best to delay it until quite late to avoid the problem of people avoiding work until the Stand Up Meeting.

   • Don't let the nit pickers pick their nits. Coaches take notice.

   • If it becomes just an empty ritual, then consider an on-demand stand-up as needed. But, evaluate the effectiveness of this in your periodic **Retrospectives**.

   One useful practice at the meeting is to "take the temperature" of the iteration. The coach or tracker can ask if anyone thinks the iteration won't be completed successfully. A graphic (Information Radiator) can be drawn on the white board to represent the degree of risk of not completing all the stories successfully.

   Note that the **Onsite Customer** or **ScrumMaster** can declare an end to the iteration if business conditions make the current work obsolete or there is no point in continuing for other reasons.

   Distributed teams will find this both a difficult and an especially important practice. The team needs awareness of the work of other members.

   This practice was adopted from Scrum [18], and has become a standard XP practice. It is discussed in detail in Yip [22].

Small Releases (Incremental Development)

You are an agile team. You are planning for the near term.

???

Agile development's sweet spot is in situations in which there is a lot of uncertainty or change is likely to make plans obsolete. It therefore works on a tight feedback cycle in which you get information to permit re-steering of the project. *Feedback is impossible unless real users have a chance to see and use the system.*

• You need feedback from the **Onsite Customer** as well as the stakeholders she represents on the current project direction.

• The customer needs validation that you really **Deliver Customer Value**.

• Early decisions, if wrong, can cost you plenty later.

• Validation of small increments is easier and cheaper than trying to prove everything is ok in a large release.

! ! !

Therefore, *schedule releases of the growing system on short cycles of about one month.*

• Releases can and should come every few iterations.

• In Scrum, the release is once per sprint, which lasts one month.

• **Daily Deployment** has been successfully applied, so it is possible to be really extreme.

• You must be willing to act on the feedback and change both direction and process if necessary. It isn't a feedback loop unless something changes.

• When you get real user feedback, hold a **Retrospective** to be sure you capture the essential message.

Note that agile methodologies depend on the feedback from customers and users to guide the project. If you don't need this feedback, then agile may not be your best methodology.

Easy Does It (Don't Push Too Hard)

You are the customer on an agile team. You are deep into the **Planning Game**. You are reviewing estimates and using the velocity given by the team to schedule stories.

???

You, the customer may be too anxious to see a lot of progress. You may not entirely trust the developers to give you **Best Effort**. *If you push too hard, you are at risk of not completing anything.*

• You like low story estimates, thinking that things get done quickly.
• You like a high velocity for an iteration, thinking that a lot will get done.
• Nearly everyone wants to do a good job.
• Coercion doesn't build software. People respond poorly to coercion.
• The environment is important. A high-pressure environment seldom improves quality or motivation, especially when the pressure is external.
• There are more effective ways to keep the project moving forward smoothly than pure pressure.
• You want the team to work at its maximum sustainable pace.

! ! !

Therefore, *don't try to push the developers for low estimates or for high velocity.* Only so much work will get done in an iteration no matter what the estimates and velocities are. You are better with accurate numbers than with optimistic ones. If they cannot be accurate, due to lack of knowledge, you are better off with conservative rather than aggressive estimates.

If you try to put too much into an iteration, you run the risk of nothing being completed. Partly this is due to the fact that wise developers will both optimize over the stories in an iteration and will refactor to make it easier to build them. This takes time. If there is too much to do generally then it won't be done well and you can end the iteration with many stories partially built, but few or none completed. This will drive the velocity down for the next iteration, complicate your own planning, and generally dishearten everyone.

• If you really don't trust the developers, then work with them to develop trust. If you really can't trust the developers, then replace them. But their responsibility is the technical requirements that go into the stories, while yours is the business value.
• You will be present continually as the team works, so should be able to judge if people are slacking or giving Best Efforts.
• Let the pressure come from the developers themselves. If progress is slow hold a **Retrospective** to learn what can be changed to increase it. Coach, take notice.

Estimates that are too high by a modest amount are easier to work with than underestimates, similarly with velocities that are too low. Near the end of an iteration it is much easier and more satisfying if the team **Asks For More** work than if they need to come to you asking what should be dropped since not everything can be completed (**Graceful Retreat**). If you push too hard you put yourself in a poor position as well as leading the team to burnout, which will not improve your product or future development efforts. But even if you don't complete your tasks this iteration, you will correct in the next cycle using **Yesterday's Weather**.

Hints for success: Make a big deal of it when the developers first come to you for more work. Find some way to reward them. Make it possible for this to occur early in the project.

Be Human (Humane Workplace)

You are managing an agile team. You are setting up the environment, or you are trying to keep the process running smoothly with lots of happy and productive developers.

???

People work best when they can behave like people, not machines. People are social. *People need a variety of experience so that they don't get bored or stuck.*

• To keep people happy, balance work and life.
• Food is an important part of our social interactions.
• If people work too hard for too long they often become less effective.
• The mind works when "idle". Sometimes it is more effective when not being pushed.
• Don't underestimate the power of serendipity. Sometimes just chatting can bring out important information, opportunities, and solutions.

! ! !

Therefore, *provide a work environment that lets people interact naturally as if it were a social setting.* For example, provide food in the workspace as well as a social corner in which people can talk. Have occasional time-outs that are purely social or purely fun.

A wise manager will bring snacks into the workplace. Provide a small refrigerator for the team's use. Have a party occasionally at the end of a successful iteration. Tension breaking activities are also useful whether they involve food or games or whatever the team likes to do. Games and toys can be useful in keeping the team moving forward and happy about the work. Have ceremonies that are meaningful to the team members and reward good behavior. Let the team members find ways to reward each other.

• There is a cost in money and time, of course, but happy, rested, people think and work more effectively than those overworked and tired.
• Sugar, fat, and caffeine are not especially healthy, though these are the typical choices.
• This may be culturally dependent, of course. If your coach is knowledgeable about the local culture, she can probably help you do this appropriately.
• If you absolutely must have a high pressure environment, perhaps ASD is not your best methodology. It is based on the principle that development is a creative activity.

Note that the goal here is more than just morale. People work best when they are happy and rested. The Sustainable Pace (40 hour week) practice of XP is designed not only to create a Humane Workplace, but also to get the best work out of everyone every minute they are engaged. Development work is creative. You, the manager, need to foster the creative environment.

If you want to see the effect of this on creative work, visit an art studio. Disney

Studios was known for its pranks and tension breakers, but was both creative and productive.

Notes: the related Do Food appears in [15, pg 132] for much the same reason, though in a different context.

Sacred Schedule

You are a developer on an agile project in the development phase of an iteration.

???

If you don't end the iteration on time, you have no basis of knowing where you are. Recall that most projects are estimated as 90% done after the first third of the project and remain so until long after the due date. If you slip schedule you lose control rapidly. It becomes easy to do it again. If you fail to complete a task in the current iteration, someone is unhappy, of course, but you know where you are.

• There is pressure to finish everything, but the clock gets in the way.

• One more (hour, day, week) would let you finish all this work. But you might not finish then, either.

• If you don't know how fast you can really go, you can't plan for the future.

• With accurate velocities (story points per iteration) you can plan future iterations and releases with confidence. This lets you control cost.

• Nothing in development is really sacred, however.

! ! !

Therefore, *don't put off the scheduled end of an iteration, even for just a day.* Sprints are strictly time-boxed. Some tasks may not get completed, but this is self-correcting in your future velocities. The only work that gets counted in an iteration for the computation of the next velocity (**Yesterday's Weather**) are the tasks completed and accepted by the customer. If you didn't finish it, don't count it. This will give you a lower, but more realistic, velocity for the next iteration.

• If you don't finish a task or a story in the current iteration, you can save (but not commit) the work done and write a story for its completion with a new time estimate. The customer can schedule these or not in future iterations.

• Customers may have a hard time with this initially and require training. They like to think that the pile of stories in an iteration is like a contract. They are unhappy when you don't complete everything. If you have kept everyone informed along the way you can lessen the blow for the customer at the end. Write stories and move on. Coach, take notice.

• Plan to have the final integration test at noon of the last day of the iteration. If everything comes together nicely you can **Refactor** for half a day. Or have a party. If not, you have half a day to make it right.

• Over a few iterations you will know how much work, in story points, the team can do in (say) ten days. This gives you the basis of long-term estimation by extrapolation, as long as the average difficulty of the stories remains the same.

• However, there are situations in which the customer has a special need. There may be long-scheduled meetings with real users who have traveled a distance to try certain features. You might need to accommodate this, even if it means (gasp) putting in overtime for a short period. Management should expect lower productivity after a push, however. Sometimes it helps to reward people for the effort required in the push. Above all, however, avoid the death-march syndrome that is all too common today.

• The work completed forms the basis of long term planning by management. Once you know how many story points you can complete in an iteration you know how much work this team can get done on this project by some future date and/or how long it will take you to complete an estimated amount of work. If you slip schedule, you have no basis for this planning.

Bug Generates Test

You are a developer on an agile team, or perhaps the customer. You have just found a bug. Oh my.

???

Bugs will occur. They are an indication of inadequate testing. *When you fix a bug you want to know both that it is fixed, and that it stays fixed in the future.*

• Good programmers write few bugs, but not NO bugs. Bugs happen to good programmers. You tried, but you didn't catch everything that could possibly go wrong when you originally built the feature using **Test First**.

• Requirements are evolving. Sometimes what appears to be a bug is an inconsistency in requirements.

• You need to know how the bug is behaving and why.

• You need confidence that you have removed it.

• You don't want a solution to introduce other bugs.

! ! !

Therefore, *whenever you find a bug, create a test so that you know when you have fixed it and that it stays fixed.*

It may require several tests, actually, but the tests you write will guide your debugging efforts.

• Like **Test First**, this is a practice that takes discipline and it may seem awkward at first.

• If you do this a lot, you probably need to improve your Test First discipline.

• If you do this a lot recently, it is probably time for a big **Refactoring** push.

• If bugs are discovered by the customer, it is a sign that communication needs to be improved. Developers may need a better understanding of the stories.

• A good set of tests written when the bug is first discovered will also help you avoid the common practice of applying a cosmetic patch, and will lead you to explore the problem more deeply.

Some bugs occur because what you built was inadequately specified. You need to learn what should have been built, of course, and capture that knowledge in tests. Some bugs occur because you built the wrong thing. But if you had adequate tests beforehand, this would not have occurred.

Note that changing requirements does not imply an error has occurred, though tests will fail as they match the old requirements, not the new. This implies that when tests fail you need to understand whether it is the code or the test that is failing. Update accordingly.

Implementer Re-estimates Task

You are a developer on an agile team and are in the Planning Game phase. Stories have been received from the customer for the iteration and have estimates. You are tasking out the stories and estimating the individual tasks.

???

Individuals take responsibility for individual tasks. Tasks are carried out by a pair (**Pair Programming**), but one person has responsibility. Commitment to the task is required for successful completion. You need commitment by the team's individuals to the work so that they are excited about what they do. More important, *the team needs accurate estimates of the time needed to perform the task.*

• People are individuals. Some are optimistic estimators, some pessimistic, though not everyone understands her own abilities.

• On the other hand, if someone is interested in a task it is likely that she knows something about it and is therefore the best person to provide an estimate, both because she knows the work and because she knows herself.

• Fine-grained estimation like this can seem chaotic. You want a **Social Tracker**.

• It will be hard to gain appropriate commitment if task estimates are assigned by others. That practice can also lead to the hardest tasks not finding any takers.

! ! !

Therefore, *when you pick up a task card to implement it, re-estimate the task.* If it doesn't agree with any existing estimate, inform the Tracker.

• Straightforward tasks are estimated quickly and accurately. More difficult situations take time and effort. Sometimes you must **Spike** to learn or split stories into tasks.

• But note that estimates are just that: estimates. They aren't perfect. They aren't perfectly accurate. Don't spend time estimating that you could use to **Deliver Customer Value**.

• Record your personal estimates and later the actual time spent in your **Project Diary**.

• The story estimate done earlier for the **Planning Game** might be rather different from the aggregate of its task estimates. This is because the story was estimated by the team and is something of a compromise. When a task is about to be performed, the person who will do it is in a position to give the best estimate of the required effort. If the total task estimate is less than the total story estimate the team can **Ask For More** work then or later. However, if the sum of task estimates is higher than that for stories you must go back to the customer and have some stories dropped from the iteration (**Graceful Retreat**). Not doing this is asking for trouble. On the other hand, if things go well you can always **Ask**

56

For More.

      Stories, unlike tasks, are estimated by the team as a whole, and so the team owns those estimates. If the granularity of the estimates is small the stories may not need to be further broken into tasks. Often, however, this is not the case and the team "tasks out" the stories. The resulting tasks are then estimated by the individuals who chose to perform them. As a rule of thumb, if an iteration is 10 days, then a story estimate of more than 3 ideal (person) days may be too big. Sometimes the customer can break this story into parts, which will aid her in scheduling (as the parts may not have equal value). If the customer cannot do this, then the team should task it out so that as much parallel effort as possible is achieved. In general, a story whose estimate is a significant fraction of the average individual velocity is at risk of not actually fitting into the iteration. The "rule of three" stated above is a bit conservative, but you would rather be safe. Experience will give you a better number at which you start to worry.

Estimate Whole Task

You are a developer in the **Planning Game** of an agile project. You are estimating a story or task.

???

When you build something, to do it successfully, you must test it properly. You must understand it properly and document it. In agile development, all this is critical due to the highly iterative nature of the process and the changing requirements. But talking to the customer, testing, and infrastructure work take time. *Everything is the "most important" thing.*

• Many tasks have necessary prerequisites that haven't been explicitly stated in any story. If they must be done, they must be estimated and the customer involved.

• Testing, for example, will take you a significant fraction of the time it takes to build a task. You may write more code for the tests than is needed for the task itself.

• Testing in ASD is not an extra task. It is part of every task.

• **Documentation Is Just Another Task** that must be done for every story.

• You need to talk to the customer to refine the few sentences on the story card into a real understanding of the underlying requirement. This takes time.

• You may need to **Spike** to understand the requirement or how to implement it.

• **Refactoring** to improve the code and make a story easier to build takes time.

• However, you will be tempted to estimate only the obvious things in the press of time.

• Slight overestimates are easier to live with in time-boxed development than underestimates.

• And you want to plan so that keeping the **Sacred Schedule** will be possible.

! ! !

Therefore, *include in your estimates of stories and tasks the time needed for all the work that supports the story. This includes, for example, time to test the feature, integrate it, and document it.*

• Some things, like testing, recur in every story. Some things are unique.

• It can be hard to think of everything, of course. When you err, you may need to re-estimate. This may cause you to go back to the customer for a **Graceful Retreat**. Customers don't like it when this occurs.

• If you find your team underestimating stories, be sure to address this specifically in the **Retrospectives**.

Testing stories may require you to write some test fixtures for a tool like FIT or FitNesse so that the customer (or **Customer-Tester Pair**) can write the actual tests. Unit testing in JUnit requires writing the actual tests. Include all of this in your estimates. Keep records on how effective you are at this estimation by keeping a record of velocity in your **Project Diary**. These records can help you improve if you refer to them when you next have to make an estimate. **Flexible Velocity** sometimes works as a stopgap when you fail to set aside enough time.

The estimate includes the time that will be required for any activity that must be completed to successfully build the story. This might include time to set up some required infrastructure, though it might be best to separate that out as a separate story. Certainly time required to **Refactor** existing code to aid implementation of a new story must be included in that story's estimate. Note, however, this implies that the story estimate must change over time, and that estimates done long ago have less certainty than they did when made. For this reason we **Re-estimate Periodically**.

Testing tools: http://fitnesse.org, http://junit.org, http://fit.c2.com

Team Owns Individual Velocities

You are a member of an agile team in the development phase, or you are a manager overseeing an agile team. Your **Implementers Re-estimate Tasks**, and you **Estimate Whole Task**.

???

When a developer takes responsibility for a task she estimates the (ideal) time to complete the task. Enough tasks are taken and estimated up to the developer's individual velocity for the iteration. People estimate differently. *Estimates can be a point of contention between developers and stakeholders.*

• Unless a task is very small and well defined, estimates will be inaccurate.

• Managers like to manage. They think of that as their job. They also like to use available numbers to help them. Some numbers, however, may mislead.

• Estimates affect velocity and velocity affects estimates. Both are largely independent of how much actual work can be accomplished. Individual velocity is just a measure of how much work a person can do in their own personal point scale.

• The **Social Tracker** needs to know from the individual developers the likelihood of successful completion of the iteration.

• An optimistic estimator will set low estimates, ignoring that things can go wrong because they usually don't. A pessimistic estimator will be aware of everything that could possibly go wrong and will give long estimates. Both will likely be wrong. This inaccuracy is corrected for in the team velocity. The optimistic estimator won't get as much done as she thinks. The pessimistic one will get more done than his worst-case scenario. So the optimistic estimator will tend to have lower velocities than a pessimistic one even though they may do the same work.

! ! !

Therefore, *let the team own the individual velocities. As manager, you must ignore individual velocities as they don't measure quantity or quality of work done.* Individuals keep their own velocity in their personal **Project Diary**. These may shared with the tracker to plan an iteration.

To emphasize this consider the situation in which there is a task card on the table that could be done by either John or Sue. John picks it up and estimates 3, and his velocity is 3. If he gets the task done this cycle all is well. Suppose, instead, that Sue picks up the card and estimates 7. If her velocity is 7 and she does the work in the iteration we are equally pleased. But John's velocity in the next cycle is still 3 and Sue's is still 7, though they do equal work.

• Note that keeping individual velocity is a difficult practice to maintain, as it requires discipline. The individual velocities are needed, however, so that each developer knows how much work they can reasonably commit to in an iteration. (record of velocity in the **Project Diary**)

    • Like the team velocity, the individual uses **Yesterday's Weather** to determine their velocity for the next iteration.

    • If an individual picks up too much work, it leaves the team at risk of not completing the iteration. But **Pair Programming** with the right individual can help correct in the short term. Ask for help.

    • From the individual's perspective, knowing your personal velocity and being able to accurately and consistently estimate how long it will take you to perform tasks is a skill that will pay you dividends. It is difficult for someone to coerce you into an impossible schedule if you have a reputation for accurate estimation.

    • The team's velocity on the other hand is worth tracking. It is an important planning and projection tool.

Spike

You are a developer on an agile team, perhaps the **Implementer** who **Re-estimates Tasks**. During the **Planning Game** you don't understand how to estimate a story or task or you don't know how to implement it.

???

You will often get a story or task that you don't know how to build or even how to estimate accurately. Often the best solution here is to have the customer break the story into smaller parts since it is easier to estimate small things than large. But you can also take a few minutes to a few hours to do exploratory development to see what the problems are. Wild guessing can be dangerous.

• Before you can estimate something you have to know how to do it. You need to **Estimate Whole Task** for this story.

• Usually you can learn something by building a simple prototype or by drawing out a design or playing with CRC cards or the like.

• Sometimes you need to choose between somewhat nonequivalent alternatives. The tradeoffs between them may be critical to success. But see **Just Do It**.

• Experimentation takes time and effort.

• Building the wrong thing is expensive.

• Experimental programming is fun. You can waste a lot of time doing it. But you want to **DTSTTCPW** and **Deliver Customer Value**.

! ! !

Therefore, *when you don't know how to do something build some throwaway code or create a throwaway design to investigate the issue.* This is called a "spike." You can also spike to help choose between alternatives. Sometimes the customer gets involved in choosing the solution as it affects cost and quality. Sometimes what you learn in a spike can give the customer ideas that will cause her to re-steer the project, in fact.

• Spikes are thrown away at the end and not incorporated into the build. For this reason it is sometimes appropriate for individuals (rather than pairs) to spike. It is also sometimes acceptable for a larger group to spike.

• Spikes are small and fast and probably dirty. They are not prototypes.

• If you have two or more approximately equal possible solutions, don't waste a spike on choosing one. Just pick one and get on with it. You aren't optimizing here. **Just Do It.**

• Build just enough in the spike to learn the needed lesson. Don't try to build a complete thing. That would be wasting resources.

• Time to spike is included in the estimates, though to some extent, it is also included in the difference between ideal time and real time (the velocity). But when you recognize a spike is needed, include it in the estimate.

- Spikes cost you time and money, of course, but the team needs to learn somehow.
- The daily **Stand Up Meeting** can often be used to send someone off on a spike. Make sure you bring the knowledge back to the team.

Promiscuous Programming

You are a developer on an agile team. You have responsibility for one or more tasks in this iteration. You are about to begin a task or subtask and are looking for a partner for Pair Programming.

???

The practices of ASD are synergistic. They cover the goals of any development project, but often in a different way. Common code ownership is an important practice. It helps you avoid a lot of documentation, as the team generally knows everything about the code base. *No one person should become a knowledge bottleneck with respect to any aspect of the project or its artifacts*. This implies that what one person knows, others know as well.

• Sometimes you feel more comfortable with some team members than others and you tend to choose those you favor when you pair up.
• Some team members may be considered "newbies" or "outsiders" for some reason and might not be chosen as often or might be left to pair with each other. This can cause an "us" vs. "them" schism within the team.
• Sometimes a guru is the one every team members wants to work with to ensure that deadlines are met. Or you are overawed by the guru and avoid him/her.
• You want to build trust and knowledge in the team.
• You want to be effective and have the team also be effective.
• You don't want to be left behind. But others have skills you don't.
• You want to improve your own skill and you want those with less to get up to speed.
• You don't want to be bored.
• The work environment can improve if it has some social aspects that don't interfere with the work.

! ! !

Therefore, *switch partners for every task at least. Spread the knowledge of the code and of the programmers throughout the team.* Pair with everyone repeatedly, even if it takes **High Discipline**. Track who you pair with in your **Project Diary**. Note the times as well.

• Knowledge will spread through the team.
• You become a generalist, rather than a specialist. This is a trade-off, of course, but agility depends on it.
• Often not everyone is especially compatible with everyone else. Work to overcome this. If management encourages everyone to **Be Human** it can help.
• If your team tends to form permanent cliques, then ASD may not be your best

methodology.

    • You want to encourage practices by which the least skilled among you can increase their skills rapidly and become more productive. **Pair Programming** with experts aids in this. Pairing with a wide variety of people with different skills aids in this.

    • Oddly enough there is some evidence that pairing with people unlike yourself (life history, race, sex, etc.) will teach you things you couldn't easily otherwise learn. The work of diverse teams has been shown to be higher quality than that of homogeneous teams. See Surowiecki [21].

    • There is some evidence that switching every hour is beneficial to the project. See Belshee [4]

Cards and Whiteboards

You are any member of an agile team that needs to create some artifact other than code. Perhaps this is a planning or tracking artifact. You need to keep track of where you are now and where you are going in the short term.

???

Agile projects are very fluid. *Things change all the time. People need to see what has changed.*

• Sophisticated planning tools can produce nice reports and can be good for archiving information. But you need to learn them and agree on their use.

• If you use sophisticated tools to keep track of things you will see two unfortunate things occur. First it is natural to be reluctant to throw away things that you have committed effort to creating, but this creational effort is required by sophisticated tracking tools. Second it is harder to get a team around a screen than to get them around a table picking up and rearranging cards.

• Your planning horizon is the iteration and the release. Things will change between iterations and so the current view of the release will change as you approach its completion.

• You want to encourage gesturing with the planning artifacts to make a point, scribbling quick notes on them, etc.

• If you don't keep an **Informative Workspace**, you wont know if you are on track without expending additional efforts needlessly.

! ! !

Therefore, *make the main planning and tracking tools simple, tactile, visible, and non-technological. Paper is good.* Stories are written on small cards, not put into some tool. You want to be able to throw away mistakes without guilt. Cards are tacked to the wall. Whiteboards are equally good, as they can easily be changed as the situation changes. Make the workspace itself informative [2] so that anyone in the room can immediately see progress and problems. Make sure that housekeeping knows not to erase your whiteboards, of course.

• If your team is dispersed then it may be necessary to use electronic means, but you will pay a cost for this. Keep such electronic documents in a common electronic workspace and make sure everyone can edit these: common ownership of all artifacts.

• The customer owns the story cards, by the way. They must be tracked; by name or number.

• Story cards and other important artifacts should not leave the workspace.

• Yes, things can get lost. This is a risk. You may want a backup electronic copy. Make sure it is clear which is the original and which is just backup.

• Note that Scrum tends to use spreadsheets, but is careful to make them visible, accessible, and modifiable.

  • As your team grows, this will be harder to do. Do what you must, but keep an **Informative Workspace**. The technological solution will cost you something, however, so make sure you watch for entropy in the **Retrospectives**.

  The author was recently coaching a team in which a very helpful tracking tool was a hand-drawn thermometer on a whiteboard. It measured the "temperature of the build" and represented the probability that the iteration wouldn't finish successfully. This also kept everything visible.

Documentation Is Just Another Task

You are a member of an agile team. You recognize that internal or external documentation is required. You also recognize that most traditional documentation isn't needed here. You will need documentation, both user level and system level. You have not gathered all the requirements up front, but you need to document requirements as well as decisions made.

???

Some people believe that documentation isn't done on agile projects. This is not true, but the documentation is different. You must do user-level documentation, of course, on any project. It may be necessary to have a separate view of the project readable by non-programmers. In agile development these are not prepared in advance, as the project direction will change. They are not prepared after the fact as people forget what was done. *You must prepare all necessary documentation and you must keep it in sync with the evolving project even as it changes.*

• The project requirements are changing constantly.
• If you leave documentation to the end, it won't get done, or will get done poorly.
• If documentation is not consistent with what you have built it is worse than worthless.
• Your build unit is the story. Your horizon is the iteration.
• You need to **Estimate Whole Task** to build the story completely. Otherwise documentation will become the orphan child of the project.
• Agile teams themselves need less documentation than other teams due to the **Executable Tests**.

! ! !

Therefore, *treat documentation creation and updating as just another task. Estimate it and refactor it as you would a programming task.* A small project can keep most of its documentation on cards and on the whiteboards. A large project can use documentation specialists on the team who work with other developers (pairing) in the usual way. A smaller team can treat documentation as a role, just like testing is. The documentation tasks may follow slightly in time the other development tasks, but not by more than a few days. User level documentation must be brought to sync at the release points.

• When a project changes direction, the documentation, like the code, must change or be discarded. This means you spent money that you might not have had to spend if you knew better earlier. It is a sunk cost, however. Move on in the best direction you can with the knowledge you now have.
• Your project isn't driven by the documentation prepared in advance. You have the

customer to steer and the code and tests to tell you what you have done.

• There is implied coordination here, and that requires communication. Those writing documentation work with the customer, as does everyone on the team.

• Code is still the best documentation for the team, assuming it is clean and well-factored. Others need a different and/or higher level view.

In an agile project the code itself is considered to be the key piece of documentation. Make sure it fits that role by always writing the code in the clearest possible way. While this is important in any project, it is essential in an agile project.

In general, remember that the **Whole Team** must include all necessary skills to build a quality product. This includes documentation skills. Note that Acceptance Tests are a form of executable documentation.

For more on Agile Documentation, see Rueping [18].

Question Implies Acceptance Test

You are customer on an agile team. Someone has just asked you a question about the meaning of a story. You want your answer to be faithfully captured by the development process.

???

If the answers to questions aren't captured reliably and accurately, the answer could get lost or misinterpreted. But the target is moving and the project is continuously re-aimed via customer steering.

• Developers ask questions of the **Onsite Customer** continuously throughout the development process. There are a lot of questions and answers.

• Answers to some questions invalidate answers to questions previously asked.

• But it takes time and effort to capture everything. Sometimes the simplest things require the most discipline, though more complicated things require the most effort.

• If requirements become inconsistent you need the inconsistencies to show up dramatically and early.

• The project may never develop sufficient traditional requirements documentation to drive a traditional black box test.

! ! !

Therefore, *whenever you, the customer, answer a question on a story or task, immediately create an acceptance test that will verify that the answer is codified in the resulting application.* The best way is to make this an **Executable Test**, but in some cases the customer will need to resort to a special card, a **Test Card**. Then a programmer can generate a test from the card. The Test Card should stay with the story that generated the question.

An absolute requirement for successful agile development is an adequate set of Acceptance Tests so that both customers and developers can agree on the target and when it is reached.

If your organization has a Quality Assurance department they can be helpful in showing the customer how to build the Acceptance Tests as you go. A testing expert on the team is a real asset.

• Note that answers to questions can also be captured in unit tests in many cases. But unit tests get refactored along with the code and are owned by the developers, not the customer. There is some danger of losing an answer if they are only captured in unit tests.

• This practices takes time and discipline. It may require that someone make an Executable Test to capture this answer. If your acceptance testing framework is really solid, the customer may be able to do it himself. Otherwise see **Customer-Tester Pair**.

Acceptance Tests are under the control of the customer or product owner. She may or may not be comfortable writing the tests directly and may need constant assistance of a team member to formulate these in an executable way. Tools such as FIT and FitNesse can help if the team can work out a way to express the tests in tabular form. Most people with business skills are comfortable thinking in spreadsheets and such tools can then be used to directly capture the test requirements.

For more on acceptance testing see Mugridge and Cunningham [17].

Re-estimate Periodically

You are a developer on an agile team. You have a bit of time available in the development phase.

???

Normally you estimate stories long before they are built. But you do so making certain assumptions. *These assumptions change and so estimates become obsolete as the application gets built and the code base changes.*

• What you originally thought to be easy may now be hard to integrate into the code base.

• What you originally thought to be hard may now be easy as you have support for it already in the code.

• You may know more than you did when you first estimated the story. It may have a different meaning now than it did earlier.

• The customer needs good estimates of stories to balance the cost against the current value. These are used for both long (project) and short (iteration, release) term planning.

• As always, you need to **Estimate Whole Task**, but this changes as you **Refactor**.

! ! !

Therefore, *in every iteration, take some time to re-estimate a few of the stories that the customer believes to be high value.* Do this only for stories with estimates that may be somewhat dated. It will be easier to know that you need to do this if you keep an **Informative Workspace**.

• Sometimes people have a bit of time because their forward progress is stopped while waiting for another task to complete, if they have finished their tasks and there are none left that will fit in the remaining time. This time can be productively spent **Spiking** and re-estimating.

• The estimates, combined with the team velocity, are the basis for long-term projection for project management. The average story estimate is an important projection tool as long as it is reasonably accurate.

• Failing to have estimates that accurately reflect the current understanding of the project will greatly complicate the **Planning Game** and make planning a long and arduous task, rather than the half-day or so per month that it should be. Do just enough of this to smooth the next Planning Game. The customer can guide you here, by indicating the likely stories in the near future.

• But don't agonize over the estimates. If you aren't sure, you can **Spike** now or later and you can always make a consciously high estimate to cover uncertainty. Another strategy when estimation is hard is to split stories.

• If you find you seldom do this and the **Planning Game** often bogs down for poor/outdated estimates, you need to deal with the issue in the next Retrospective and set a **Flexible Velocity**.

For more on agile estimation, see Cohn [7].

Flexible Velocity

You are a **Social Tracker** for an agile team. The team recognizes that there is work to do that is not covered by the stories. You are in the **Planning Game** working on the next iteration.

???

Sometimes the stories to be included in an iteration have implications that are not obvious to the customer. They may require **Refactoring** or infrastructure development. *Work may need to be done that is not covered in any of the stories.*

- Setting an appropriate velocity for the iteration is the key to success. If it is too high, the developers will have to drop work in the iteration, making everyone unhappy.
- We want everything stated in the stories. We want to **Estimate Whole Task**.
- In practice this won't always happen. You aren't perfect.
- You may need to do some things to support current stories (not future possibilities). These extra tasks were not captured in the estimates, though they should have been.
- The velocity needs to accurately estimate what the team can reasonably do in the iteration.
- As always, it is easier and more satisfying to go back to the customer to **Ask For More** than to have to go and ask for a **Graceful Retreat**.

! ! !

Therefore, *adjust the velocity downwards for an iteration in which you know that there is work to be done that isn't included in any of the stories.*

This extra work can be **Refactoring** the existing code since the stories might have been estimated at an earlier time and the current state of the code base implies refactoring. Alternatively (preferably) the story estimate can be updated to include this Refactoring.

Some teams use *developer stories* to cover this situation. They are estimated and scheduled in the normal way, but they are inserted into the mix just in time by the developers to support a customer story. Don't use them to speculate what might be coming in the future and build code speculatively. **DTSTTCPW**, of course. But there will likely be arguments between the customer and the developers over the priority, and even the need for, developer stories as they aren't well understood by most customers.

- Note that in ASD we do the simplest thing that could possibly work. This does not mean we hack. It does mean that we do not build the most general solution to every problem when we first encounter it. It is the second or third occurrence of a problem that pays for the general solution. Since you don't know the order in which the stories will be built when you first estimate them, it is hard to write estimates that include this time to refactor. This is one reason why velocity stays at a fraction of available time, of course, but it also sometimes requires adjustments to the velocity of an iteration.

• If you **Estimate Whole Task** accurately for each story then the need for this should not occur. This is a temporary stopgap. Discuss the problem in your next **Retrospective**.

• Be aware that the customer won't like it when this happens. The long-term solution is to try to get more complete estimates for the stories and their implications.

• Management will need to merge infrastructure requirements smoothly into the development. Make sure the required equipment does arrive in time and that you know who will set it up and check it out.

This extra work can include necessary infrastructure work needed to support a story. On a recent project, the velocity stayed at about one-third of available time (the organization has frequent required meetings), but hardware infrastructure was poorly planned and didn't get accounted for in story estimates. Velocity had to be reduced to get the machines up and running.

Once And Only Once

You are a developer on an agile team. Development is proceeding. You are coding a task.

???

Often when you are coding in an iterative environment, you notice that you are writing a piece of code that you have written before. If you **DTSTTCPW** then you are likely to just repeat it or cut-paste for the new code. *Redundancy costs you in maintainability*, however. When the system changes in the future, all redundant copies must be brought into sync and the tools are not very helpful in finding the places that need update.

- You want simple code that is easy to write.
- You want good code that is easy to maintain.
- You want elegant code that is easy to modify.
- The above are often in conflict.
- Requirements are likely to change as any agile project proceeds.
- Building code more elegant than necessary wastes money.
- You have tests to tell you it is correct. Your skill should tell you if it is ugly.

! ! !

Therefore, *when you refactor, bring the redundancies together using an appropriate object/functional design.*

- However, don't anticipate this need. Remember that it is the second (or third) use that pays for generality. You may need to revisit code that you are writing now, but you may not. Building in unnecessary generality at every chance is expensive and wasteful. Pay the price when you must, but only when you must.
- Recognizing this situation takes some practice, as does solving it. If you find it difficult to do this in some case, examine your overall coding practice. If your redundancy is at the level of switches it is harder to handle than if it is at the level of method bodies.
- **DTSTTCPW** is not an excuse to hack. Don't let your code go out of coherence. But don't pay for generality that may not be needed. In most cases **YAGNI**.
- Like the "first rule of optimization", the first rule of generalization in an agile project is "Don't do it". The second rule, for experts, is "Don't do it, yet." I learned this from Ledgard, but it is really due to Michael Jackson.
- This is from Beck, *Smalltalk Best Practice Patterns*[3].

There is a lot more to **Constant Refactoring** than Once And Only Once, but it is a good place to start.

Note that while the above has been stated in terms of code, it can also be applied to other created artifacts, such as designs and tracking documents.

Continuous Integration

You are a developer on an agile team. You have just finished the development of a story or task and all of the unit tests pass.

???

Stories are broken into tasks unless they are already very small. It is the tasks that are assumed and built by the developers. Unit tests are written at the task (and sub task) level. *If you don't integrate the task into the build you won't know early enough that you have a problem.*

• Many projects fail because they are built from parts that won't integrate at the end.
• Small assumptions made frequently by many people accumulate into large problems.
• Integration takes time. It often invalidates your assumptions.
• Small bits of code are easier to integrate than large ones.
• But with many pairs working, integration can be a bottleneck.
• Task integration requires good code management tools such as CVS and SVN unless the team is very small. (http://www.nongnu.org/cvs/, http://subversion.tigris.org/)

! ! !

Therefore, *immediately integrate every task into the build when all its unit tests pass.*

A code repository that helps you do this is essential. CVS, for example, has such capabilities. You can run (and must pass) all the tests against the code base before you commit, so that when you do, you know that nothing is broken.

• This is another job that requires discipline. The coach must be vigilant.
• Since tasks are small, integration is more likely to be successful. When not successful, the problems more likely to be manageable than when you do "big bang" integration. You also learn earlier when you have a problem if you integrate frequently. But if you can't make all the tests pass, you can't commit the code.
• Each pair of programmers may be integrating a task every day or so (more frequently in some teams). This implies discipline with respect to maintenance of the code base. An integration machine on which all integration tasks are carried out can help here.
• To emphasize: when you integrate, all the unit tests must pass. Not just the tests for this feature, all the tests. This implies, of course, that the tests are in the repository along with everything else and thus are accessible to everyone. You also need to achieve a **Ten Minute Build**.
• You also need to run the Acceptance Tests. Those for the story just built must pass, of course, but you need a policy for what happens when a new story being integrated makes an acceptance test that was passing now fail. In many teams this is a show-stopper

and all work halts until the situation is resolved.

     • You may actually need two (or more) repositories for code. One contains the committed code against which all tests pass. The other contains work in progress and is put in a centralized place only to assure that backups get done and nothing gets lost if a machine crashes or is stolen.

     • When you think you have finished a task, but nothing you do makes it integrate correctly, warn the tracker that there may be delays.

     The integration process has four parts. (1) Run all the tests against this new code. They must all pass. (2) Integrate the entire code base back into the local version. (3) Run all the unit tests for the system (the "suite"). They must all pass. (4) Commit the code back to the repository. The implication is that the code in the repository is always working integrated code. The integration process maintains the invariance of this state.

     Continuous Integration is especially difficult in distributed teams since you need to avoid conflicts as much as possible. The reduced awareness of the activities of the remote developers may lead to problems. You may need tools, and will need procedures, to be sure you have adequate awareness among team members. [19]

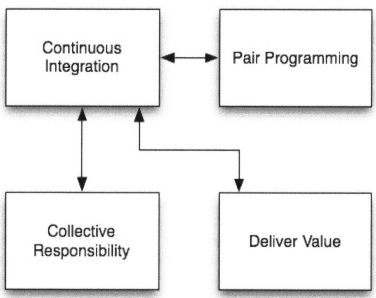

Continuous Integration

Social Tracker

You are the tracker on an agile team. Development progresses.

???

The tracker needs fine-grained knowledge of the state of the project, but the knowledge is in individual heads. As tracker, you are responsible for important guidance at the **Stand Up Meeting** every day. Most team members are too mired in the detail of their own tasks to see the bigger picture.

• If the tracker doesn't talk to everyone frequently she won't know what is going on.

• The person serving in the tracker role has other development tasks as well. Tracker is seldom a full time role. It should take less than an hour per day.

• The tracker integrates information held by the developers, but needs to visit with them to gather it.

! ! !

Therefore, *the tracker spends five minutes or so with everyone at least twice a week, preferably daily.* She needs to know if the tasks being undertaken are likely to be completed and will compile team velocity as well as the number of tests written and passing. She needs to know (a) which tasks are done , (b) which are in progress, and (c) what is the likelihood that all will be completed.

• The tracker also reports progress at the **Stand Up Meeting** and through visuals (*information radiators*) on the walls. If there is no **ScrumMaster**, she may lead the **Stand Up Meeting**.

• As with many of the agile roles, it is best if this one rotates every iteration or so. This spreads knowledge and skill.

• The tracker can maintain most of the information radiators in your **Informative Work Space**.

• The tracker can be the one to inform the customer if there is too much or too little work in the iteration. In the former case she learns from the **Onsite Customer** what should be dropped and transmits this to the developers. In the latter case she will **Ask For More** work from the customer. All of this requires knowledge of the tasks completed and those currently worked on. Early knowledge of both these situations helps the team be productive.

• Note, however, that each developer keeps track of her own velocity and progress. Tracking is not an external, or management task, but an individual information task. People will be less honest if it is seen as management control.

The tracker maintains fine-grained knowledge of the progress of an iteration. Over time this accumulates into information useful to management, such as the team velocity and the number of tests written, etc.

Note: I hesitated to call this one Promiscuous Tracker.

Note also that *Done* means more than coded. A task must be thoroughly tested, documented, integrated into the code base and accepted by the customer before it can be called done. See **Estimate Whole Task**.

Project Diary

You are a developer on an agile team. You are building code to implement stories and tasks .

???

Individual velocity figures must be known and accurate. If you don't know how fast you can go, you won't know how much work you can pick up.

• The only way to learn to estimate well is to do it and to record a history of your estimates and the resulting actual times.

• The team estimates are based ultimately on individual estimates.

• Agile development can't function if estimates can't be depended on or are inconsistent.

• Recording takes discipline. The coach can be a nag here. Every task should be recorded.

• With self-reflection, based on data, a person can learn a lot about how they estimate: optimistic, pessimistic, or generally accurate. Being optimistic or pessimistic isn't necessarily bad, but it is useful to know how your estimates compare with the actual time you take.

! ! !

Therefore, *each developer keeps a bound book for the project in which estimates and resulting actual times are recorded for each task.* The book should say something about the nature of each task and the times need to be in the same (ideal) terms. To do this you must record the ideal time you spend on each task, not just the elapsed time.

• Your record book will help you become a better estimator over time if it is accurate, up to date, and consulted while you are estimating the next task or story.

• Estimation, like swimming, is not a skill you learn by thinking about it. You have to practice it. Initially your estimates will be terrible, but make them, just to give yourself a baseline. You won't improve your estimates unless you record them so that you can look back over how you estimated similar things in the past. The record can also tell you if you are a generally optimistic or a pessimistic estimator.

• The estimation book of a developer should be considered her property. The numbers in it are not useful for planning or evaluation of the employee. The tracker keeps a book for the team.

• Theme books are good for this. They help assure that pages don't disappear since they have a sewn binding.

This practice is drawn from PSP (Personal Software Process)[9]

Velocity is the relationship between ideal and real time. Project and individual velocity is never the same between individuals or between projects. They differ widely depending on the individual, the organization, and the work. In some organizations, people normally spend half their time in meetings and on tasks other than the development tasks that are nominally their main job description. Therefore, don't try to compare your velocity to that of another project, team, organization, or individual.

Customer Checks-Off Tasks

You are the **Onsite Customer** on an agile development team. Developers have come to you with a "completed task" for your approval.

???

Tasks must be checked off only when done. Otherwise you will miss things. The **Onsite Customer** is the judge of what is done.

• When a task is completed it is checked off (and a small celebration ensues.) However, if the developer checks off the task when she thinks she is done, there is room for disagreement.

• A task isn't done until the customer is satisfied.

• If developers think it is done and it isn't, then they will find integration difficult, though perhaps not immediately.

• If developers think it is done, but you, the customer, are out of the loop they may drift toward assuming what you want.

• It needs to be clear to all when a task is done.

• Done doesn't mean coded. It means coded, tested, integrated, documented, etc. See **Estimate Whole Task**.

! ! !

Therefore, when the developer is "done" with a task, she takes it to the customer for a demo. The customer will run any Acceptance Tests on the task (or write and run them if this has been neglected). *When the customer is satisfied, the customer checks off the task as done.*

• Note that if the developer thinks a task is done and the customer disagrees there may be a problem with understanding of the task. The customer can accept the task, but write new stories to correct it and schedule these in the usual way. The customer can also reject the task. If there is time in the current iteration to satisfy the customer, do so, otherwise you will need to discard the work and let the customer reschedule. This affects current velocity, of course. Don't count work not accepted in the computation of **Yesterday's Weather**.

• Avoid blame when tasks are not accepted. Blame buys you nothing. It matters not a bit if the customer or the developer is responsible for the "failure." What is important is that you move the project forward. Stories do that. Write stories and move forward. If this happens often, make sure to seek the root cause in your **Retrospective**. There are many possible reasons, among them are not understanding the problem or trying too hard to please the customer.

• But work on communication, especially when you find that misunderstandings are frequent. This is more likely to occur when the customer is not physically present when questions arise, of course. The coach should help you with this. Work toward everyone taking responsibility for miscommunication. Customers and developers usually speak different languages, have different world views and constraints. All of this can lead to miscommunication that is no-one's fault, but everyone's responsibility to correct.

• Some claim that ASD humanizes the work environment, especially with such practices as **Sustainable Pace**. The customer, however, may be overworked. She has such a central role in steering and may need a support team to fulfill the role [16].

Customer Obtains Consensus

You are the customer on an agile development team. Your project has lots of stakeholders. Your job is to be the main guide of the project team.

???

In many projects the "customer" is a complex beast. There may be many stakeholders and constituencies outside the team that have a business interest in the project. In agile development, a single person takes the role of customer and presents the interests of all of these people and organizations to the development team. The customer is charged with complete control over what is built and the composition of features in each iteration. Another way to say it is that the customer is the one charged with making all of the business decisions, while the developers make all of the technical decisions.

- Iterations are short. The pace is fast.
- The customer must speak as one for all of these individuals and groups.
- She must be empowered by the organization to make (or at least communicate) all of the business decisions that relate to the project.
- If the developers get conflicting answers to questions or conflicting demands on what to build or the importance of features, chaos can ensue.
- The customer is responsible for keeping a coherent picture of the target. It must be shared (as you go along) with the developers.
- If the picture is incoherent, so will be the product. A single view, even if imperfect, is probably better than committee designs and trying to satisfy conflicting masters. See **Guiding Metaphor**.
- Progress will stall if the developers can't get questions answered quickly as there is no comprehensive requirements documentation.

! ! !

Therefore, *you must continuously obtain consensus, or at least consent, among all of these stakeholder groups on priorities and business value.* The developers, then, look to you as the single point at which questions can be answered and from which to take direction on what to build.

- It is essential to the team that there is only one "mind" setting the direction. Otherwise, if questions are answered inconsistently then the code will become incoherent.
- There will be many questions and the team will need answers quickly if they are to continue their forward momentum. The customer with many stakeholders needs good lines of communication to all of them.
- The customer has a lot to do and must do it quickly but accurately. This role is very intense. Since iterations are so short, questions must be answered quickly. This

implies that there will need to be a lot of rapid communication among stakeholders when there is any diversity of interest among them.

 • Precisely speaking, it isn't consensus that we need, but the stakeholders must "seem" to speak with a single voice. Consensus is preferred, of course, but the designated customer must be empowered to make decisions when consensus is not possible so that the project can progress. Perhaps grudging consent of the stakeholders is enough, but it is managed by the designated customer, not by the developers.

 • Occasionally this consensus is impossible. The stakeholders just can't agree. If this becomes a problem, see **Individual Stakeholder Budgets**.

 • Another option when customers cannot agree is to "just do something." Satisfy one of the stakeholders this iteration and then try again for consensus. This is risky, of course, but your costs continue even if everyone is idle. So, doing something, as long as it makes progress, is better than doing nothing while people argue.

 • Alternatively, you, the customer, may be able to defer a decision on a feature while people fight over it, provided you have enough other things to keep the developers busy.

 • If you think of the customer as the primary product owner, then this person becomes responsible for setting the direction. If there is disagreement about the direction of the project most of it happens outside the hearing of the development team. It doesn't go away, of course.

 It may be useful to think of the development process as a pair of funnels joined at the neck. The stakeholders sit on one side and the developers on the other, with the person fulfilling the customer role at the narrow spot. Everything goes through the customer. All the complications of the business are then presented to the team as if they were a simple, single source, thing. In any case, the customer acts as the one primary representative of all the stakeholders and is the only one authorized to give direction to the developers. As such he or she is a full, indeed essential, member of the **Whole Team**.

Individual Stakeholder Budgets

You are managing an agile development team and have learned that it is not possible for the **Customer** to **Obtain Consensus** among the stakeholders.

???

*Sometimes it is impossible for a **Customer** to **Obtain Consensus**.* There may be stakeholders with conflicting goals in the process or you may have insufficient resources to satisfy everyone.

- The customer may not be able to gain consensus from among the stakeholders.
- There may be too many or too diverse a set of stakeholders.
- You still have to make progress and please the stakeholders in any case.
- Not moving forward while people fight isn't very productive.
- Giving everyone a little of what they need now may help them.

! ! !

Therefore, *in each iteration, break up the velocity into individual budgets for each stakeholder that must be satisfied.* Let each segment choose stories of most value to itself. Sometimes the stakeholders themselves can agree on an equitable distribution. Otherwise, allocation among the stakeholders must be done by some *big boss*, or the customer representative, not by the developers.

- It is hoped that the application of this is rare. It complicates planning greatly. It can also complicate integration of the various pieces that weren't integrated as you go along, having been under the control of different minds.
- This may imply, in some situations, satisfying only one stakeholder at a time, leaving the others to wait for later iterations.
- Note: This pattern is used "when all else fails." If you can convince the customer herself to do this job, you will be better off as the discussions will move outside the hearing of the developers, causing less disruption.
- If in your planning you recognize this as likely to occur, agile development may not be your best methodology. You might need to split into several projects rather than try to coordinate disagreements as you go along.

Note. This is a specialized pattern that may apply or not, depending on the number and alignment of the stakeholders. Sometimes it is very important, due to the complexity of the business framework of most software development today. It is far better when the **Customer Obtains Consensus**.

Simple Design (Incremental Design)

You are a developer on an agile team. You have some functionality to build into the existing application.

???

Design takes time. *Sophisticated design takes a lot of time and thought. But that costs money.*

• You don't have all of the requirements for the project in hand. They will likely change in any case.

• Designs are not the product. Their only value is in helping you build and maintain the product.

• If the requirements change enough, early design decisions will become invalidated. The design will need to be redone.

! ! !

Therefore, *use the simplest design you can think of that takes account of what you know at the time.*

• Don't anticipate that you know something. Don't anticipate that some story will eventually appear. Design for what you know to be true, not for what might be true in the future. But don't ignore the necessary. For example, if the scaling of a product is known (a non-functional requirement), you must design for it.

• A simple design is likely more flexible, in any case.

• By choosing an agile methodology, the team has decided to pay for this added flexibility.

• If the current design must change to accommodate the new feature, morph the design as little as is reasonable.

• Improve the design when you **Refactor**.

• If the design starts to seem chaotic, discuss it at the next **Retrospective**.

Coding Standard

You are a developer on an agile team. You need to work closely with the other developers.

???

*To achieve **Collective Ownership** and enable **Constant Refactoring**, the structure, look, and feel of the code needs to be clear to every developer.*

• Even small irritants can add to frustration.

• On an agile team, even more than in other cases, the code is read frequently by many people.

! ! !

Therefore, *adopt a common coding style that everyone agrees to use consistently.*

• The details of the style matter less than the agreement and discipline to use it.

• Tools can help.

• Naming styles and conventions are a part of this. **Pair Programming** will help you keep to a style.

Collective Ownership (Shared Code)

You are a developer on an agile team. You want to change some existing code to facilitate your current work.

???

The code on a project is a company resource, but individuals come and go. *You need to assure that more than one person is familiar with every part of the code base.*

• Developers don't like to get stuck waiting for others to act.

• Strong egos can get in the way of cooperative work.

• If knowledge is closely held in the minds of single individuals, the enterprise is at risk if the individuals should leave for any reason.

• An organization in which an individual's only security is what they know that the person in the next cubicle doesn't, is dysfunctional.

! ! !

Therefore, *assume that all code is commonly held.* If you need to change something to progress, go ahead and change it. No permission is needed from the originator.

• A consequence for management is that code tracking to individuals is impossible. The team is responsible for its code, not the individual.

• Collective ownership leads to collective reward. This strengthens teams, but is foreign to some organizations. See **Collective Responsibility**.

• Another consequence is that individuals are pushed in the direction of being generalists, rather than specialists.

• This requires a common **Coding Standard**, of course.

Ask For More

You are a developer on an agile team. You have just finished the development of a story or task and all of the unit tests pass. You realize that there is too little outstanding work in the sprint backlog to fill up the time until the end of the iteration.

???

The stories accepted for an iteration are not a contract to complete it. The estimates are only that. But, the business side needs to know how fast the team can **Deliver Customer Value** in the steady state. This enables projection and budgeting. *Therefore, wasting time when you have no task is not helpful.*

- Sometimes things go worse or better than what you expected.
- A wise customer will have a set of ready tasks in the backlog.

! ! !

Therefore, *when the team is likely to finish the stories before the end of the current iteration, ask the **Onsite Customer** for more work.*

- The **Social Tracker** should know when more work is possible. She will need to project everyone's work over the iteration to know this early enough to have an impact.
- To enable steady-state velocity tracking you will need to be sure that all work is captured in stories. This will lessen the tendency to "catch up" on work not in the Stories when you finish the scheduled tasks. That would give a false picture of how fast the team can go.
- The customer will need to know how much work to give. Give the customer a new velocity and let her choose tasks up to that value.
- The customer needs to know what work to give. The product backlog is kept in priority order, of course, so this should be easy to determine.

The wise manager will give a reward to whoever first Asks For More in the project.

Graceful Retreat

You are in an iteration and realize that you have taken on too much work and not all can be completed.

???

An iteration in which nothing is finished is extremely disruptive.

• Estimates aren't perfect and you often learn things are harder than you thought.
• There isn't perfectly accurate and complete communication between **Onsite Customer** and developer.
• Sometimes disaster strikes a team member and they cannot continue to contribute.
• The customer knows best what are the needs of the organization. She is the arbitrator of what is to be built.
• You want to complete as much work as possible in the current iteration.

! ! !

Therefore. *Let the customer decide what to finish and what to drop.*

• Velocity will drop, of course. The **Onsite Customer** and the manager may not be happy.

The typical scenario here is to go to the customer as soon as the **Social Tracker** suspects a problem. Present what has been completed, what is in process, and what is yet to be started. The customer then gives one-time advice about how to spend the developer resources to complete the iteration. Remember that we value only completed work and only things that are truly done (built, tested, integrated, documented) count in the velocity. So work hard to reach "done" on as much as possible.

The dropped work can be rescheduled as the customer desires in any future iteration (not necessarily the next). It may need to be re-estimated, of course.

Note that the response to learning you have taken on too much work is not to do a development death march to complete the work. This will skew your velocity measure, making it impossible for management to track the team and the project. Velocity for this iteration will be lower, of course, but the velocity will truly measure what this team can do on this project.

Do the Simplest Thing That Could Possibly Work (DTSTTCPW)

You are a developer on an agile team. You need to build some functionality.

???

On an agile project you don't know all of the consequences of decisions you make early. The requirements are gathered just in time. The requirements change over time. *You will waste resources if you build things that won't be needed later.*

• You want to **Deliver Customer Value**.

• Completely general solutions to a problem can be complex.

• An over-built solution costs the customer money, both initially and in maintenance.

• If you revisit an issue on a future story, you can add generality.

• If you never need to revisit an issue, the simple solution is clean and cheap.

• Code in agile projects is meant to be malleable and to be refactored.

• Something may seem important now, but changes in direction can make it obsolete before the project ends. This is why we need to be agile, actually: things change.

! ! !

Therefore, *when faced with a decision on what to do, do the simplest thing that could possibly work with what you know now.*

• This does not mean hacking.

• This does not mean ignoring known needs.

• But it does mean programming with a high degree of skill.

• If you have two possible solutions to a problem, don't spend much time deciding between them. Choose one and get on with it. Prefer the simple one. **Just Do It**.

• Simple here also means clean and easily understood. Think poetry.

The mantra is: "Just enough, just in time"

You Ain't Gonna Need It (YAGNI)

You are a developer on an agile team, building some functionality. You have some choices to make about how to proceed.

???

Traditional projects normally spend time at the beginning building needed infrastructure to support the project: tools, databases, etc. *But on an agile project, you don't know the requirements at the beginning and they are likely to change.*

• Decisions made early are expensive as you have little information on which to base them.

• If needs change, early infrastructure development can be made obsolete.

• If you know a lot about the requirements early on and they are stable, you can optimize a lot, but this is seldom true today. Throwing away infrastructure is expensive.

! ! !

Therefore, *when given a choice about something that might be necessary in the future, assume you ain't gonna need it. Build infrastructure only when you know it is required, and then only just enough.*

• Architecture must be built as you go. It must evolve with the requirements. This is a new skill for most developers.

• But if you know you do need it, then build it. Don't ignore reality.

• Delaying expensive decisions saves you money twice. You hold your money longer and you have better information to support the decision later.

• But you suffer an opportunity loss if things don't change.

• **Test First** development helps here, since you only build enough to pass a test.

Constant Refactoring

You are a developer on an agile team. You are implementing some functionality (a story) and realize that it will be difficult to do, given the current code-base.

???

Since you haven't had all the requirements at the beginning, you don't have an overall architecture or design. *The code can become a hodge-podge if it isn't carefully managed.*

- You want clean code and a good design, given what you know now.
- If the code is clean and an incremental change is small it shouldn't take a lot to cleanly integrate them, leaving the code clean. But it does take discipline.
- If the code is messy then any change is likely to leave it messy.

! ! !

Therefore, *continuously improve the structure of the code as you go.*

- Sometimes the easiest way to implement a story is to spend some time changing the existing code so that the new story fits more cleanly into it.
- If the project has to make a radical change of direction you will have high cost here, but this is because of the new requirements, not that you didn't anticipate them in an early design.
- Design patterns are a good place to look for refactoring advice and guidance. See Kerievsky[13], for example.
- If you find velocity decreasing (**Yesterday's Weather**) it is probably time to spend extra effort on refactoring. You may need to apply a **Flexible Velocity** to achieve this.

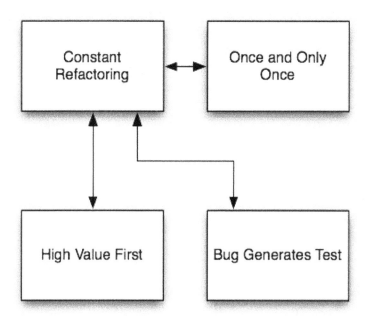

Constant Refactoring

Negotiated Scope Contract

You are a development team negotiating with a client (customer organization) for the establishment of a project. You want to create a win-win situation for the project.

???

You need effective ways to plan out the project so that both the stakeholders and the developers can be successful. You are taking on risk when you begin a project and you need to manage it. *You can't control everything, try as you might.*

• Over specified systems fail. Serendipity happens, but seldom.

• You need to control what you can and plan for what you can't control.

• Trying to over-control all the variables leaves you little room for error. The "perfect" PERT chart has every operation on a critical path.

! ! !

Therefore, *plan to control only money, time, and quality. Features are the dependent variable. Use planning, not control, to build the right thing.*

• Initial planning can be done as usual to scope the project. After a few iterations, team velocity will tell you where you can get to for a given amount of time and money.

• You may not get everything you hoped for at the beginning, but by steering the project incrementally through the iterations using **High Value First**, you can get what you most need at an acceptable cost.

Many large projects spend a disproportionate amount of time and money on low value features that someone thought "might be needed" when the product was finally delivered. Much COTS software is filled with unneeded and unused features.

Energized Work

You are a **Sheltering Manager** for an agile team. You need to set work conditions for the team

???

*You need to assure that everyone on the team gives their **Best Effort** all the time and that their effort is effective.*

- Programming is a kind of thinking. It isn't typing.
- Exhausted people never perform at their best.
- Exhausted people don't interact well with one another, but agile development depends on intense cooperative work.
- As a manager you have a right to everyone's best work every minute they are engaged in the task.
- Employees have a right to a rich personal life.
- Giving your brain a rest by doing something physical is often the best way to make progress on a difficult problem. The brain is a powerful tool if you don't abuse it.
- Tracking agile projects depends on having a stable work force with which to measure team velocity.
- Unfortunately, many teams have many tasks, all of "priority one."

! ! !

Therefore, *establish a work-day and work-week of reasonable length.* Experience has shown that this is 36-40 hours. Overtime should be very rare and only to cover an unusual short-term need, such as a scheduled demonstration to stakeholders.

- This pattern implies, and was originally called, "40 Hour Week". Those forced to work 60 hours don't just lose efficiency for the last 20, but are sub-optimal throughout their work.
- Rested, energized, developers create better code because they put in fewer defects and they spend less time removing them. There is no trade-off here. Less is more.
- Many difficult technical problems have been solved by "giving it a rest."
- The length of the work-week is, perhaps, less important here than the idea of finding ways for personal re-generation.
- There are organizations in which the culture dictates long hours for anyone wishing to be successful or to advance. These are dysfunctional organizations.
- It isn't an advantage to an organization to produce a great product and then have its team immediately quit, or be so burned-out that they are useless for the next big thing.
- When people work variable hours in a week, the velocity becomes meaningless for long term tracking and projection of the work the team can do.

• Since you work on **One Project**, other work tasks don't constitute a "break." Do something not work related to refresh your mind.

A short "push" to meet a special deadline is ok, but don't expect the same level of work immediately afterwards.

Sustainable Pace

You are any member of an agile team, but primarily the Manager.

???

You want your team to be effective for the long haul, months after month. Pushing the team too much on schedule may seem like a good thing, but it will cost you in the long term.

- When people are tired they seldom produce their **Best Efforts**
- Development is intellectual work. Your head needs to be clear to do it.
- Exhausted people often don't behave well.
- People want to give their best and will work hard without goading.
- Over specifying is counterproductive and nearly always fails.

! ! !

Therefore, *pace the team for the long haul, not a sprint.* You want everyone working in top form all the time

- An occasional burst of overtime is ok, but don't expect that it can continue without degradation of the team and its product. But a stable velocity is your best tool for projecting.

See **Energized Work** for more on this. In fact there has been an evolution here. These ideas were originally captured in the idea of a *40-Hour Week* [2]. This morphed into the ideas expressed here. The best formulation is in **Energized Work**.

Pair Programming

You are a developer on an agile team. Development is proceeding. You are coding a task.

???

When you work alone, you often get stuck. You also make simple, but possibly devious and costly, errors. You need to assure that the code is of high quality and is efficiently created.

• Code walk-throughs are typically used to assure quality but they are expensive and not an efficient use of most people's time. Everyone hates them.

• Errors introduced into code slow you down more than most anything else, as they need to be removed, but it is difficult to do so.

• Two people working on the same problem at the same time rarely get stuck simultaneously.

• Without extensive documentation, you need to spread knowledge of the code base throughout the developers on the team.

! ! !

Therefore, *whenever you write code to be committed to the code-base, do it with a partner.* Two people share one keyboard and screen. One person controls the keyboard and mouse at any given instant and the other observes and comments, but the roles switch.

• This practice is synergistic with many of the other practices, receiving and giving mutual support. It also provides you safety when a person leaves the team, as their knowledge doesn't depart with them. Skill transfer is also an asset to the organization.

• Experience has shown that the *driver* (controlling the keyboard) tends to think in a short-term tactical manner and the *navigator* tends to thing strategically about how this piece fits into the greater whole. This can improve not only error rates, but also design.

• Research has shown dramatic drops in defect rates with Pair Programming. Research has also shown little, if any, drop in productivity.

• It isn't just two that people work together. Pairs shift constantly. See **Promiscuous Programming**.

• A pair can get stuck, of course, but if you also do all your work in **Our Space** then this is even less likely to occur since you can always ask others for help.

• The owner of **My Story** need not be the driver. In fact, driver-navigator roles should switch frequently and especially if one gets blocked.

• Pairing has been shown to support a **Humane Workplace**.

• In dispersed development this is still essential. See **Remote Pair**.

The author has this picture in his head of 10 people isolated in cubicles working alone, with everyone stuck on separate problems, but with the solutions all collectively known, though in the heads of those in the other cubes.

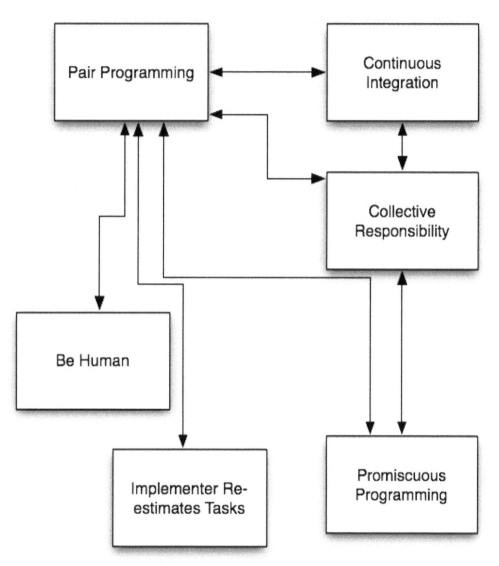

Pair Programming

Common Development Environment

You are a member of an agile team. You and the other team members are deciding on tools to use for the project

???

You and the team need to assure that people can work together seamlessly.

• People need to work closely together, such as doing **Pair Programming**, without barriers.

• People's individual preferences are less important than finding a common path to the goal. For example see **Coding Standard**.

• Every obstacle to communication will become magnified by distance and by working across time zones. Work products will need to be shared across locations.

! ! !

Therefore, *establish, from the beginning, as set of common tools and practices that everyone agrees to use.*

This is important in any project, but essential to a distributed/dispersed agile project.

Source: See Hvatum et. al. [10]

End To End

You are the **Onsite Customer** of an agile team. You are planning the first release.

???

You want to be able to measure value of the product in realistic use as early as possible.

• You need to learn enough about the feasibility early on so make rational decisions about continuing the project. But agile projects don't, normally, do extensive pre-planning.

• Pieces of a project, though complete, seldom give a realistic view of how it will all work at the end.

• There is no better judge of your product than real users.

! ! !

Therefore, *assure that the first release contains an end-to-end version of the software, usable by real users.* As customer, you can decide to actually deploy it or not.

• Not all of the functionality will be in place, of course.

• This does not imply "stub" implementations. Rather it means careful choice of stories that go into the first release so that the product hangs together from the user's standpoint, but also reveals potential technical risks.

• This end to end version sets a basic initial architecture on which the various parts can be hung.

• You need to **Think Small** to achieve this.

Distinguish between iterations and releases. It may take you several iterations to reach a release. You should **Deliver Customer Value** in each iteration, but it should be usable by real users at the release points. This gives you the opportunity for the feedback that can tell you if you need to re-steer the product. It is especially important to get this feedback early so as to validate the initial decisions of the stakeholders.

Retrospective

You are a member of an agile team. It is the end of an iteration.

???

You may need to change the process, but it might not be obvious. You want to know if the process you use is working well for you or not.

• When there is a problem, individuals may have only separate pieces of the puzzle.

• Without a clear end-to-end plan, as is typical in agile development, you need to run the project on a constant feedback stream.

• You also need to assure you keep doing the good things that are making your project a success. You want to "turn the knobs up" on the things that work.

• The team itself likely has the knowledge of what is working and what not, but you need a way to elicit this information in a safe, forward looking, manner.

• Different members of the team may have different ideas about what works and what doesn't.

! ! !

Therefore, *hold a formal retrospective[14] to determine (a) what went well and should be repeated and (b) what caused difficulties and how you should change practices to do better.*

• Important times to hold Retrospectives are at the end of the first iteration, the end of each release, and whenever the **Stand Up Meeting** reveals serious problems.

• The first few Retrospectives you do should have the assistance of a trained facilitator and require at least a day.

• Everyone needs to know from the beginning that part of the job is to be evaluative of the effectiveness of the practices.

• Retrospectives need to include the **Whole Team**.

• Retrospectives don't assign blame when things go wrong. Everyone needs to take responsibility.

• Retrospectives don't directly **Deliver Customer Value**, so they need to be kept short and goal directed. If you hold them frequently, they can take as little as an hour.

• Hold a longer Retrospective at the end of the project, of course, so that you don't lose the important lessons.

• The Respective gives advice to the **Whole Team**, not the managers. You have a **Self-Organizing Team**, after all.

Test Card

You are a customer on an agile team or an acceptance testing specialist working with the customer. You have a new story, or a new question about an existing story, for which the acceptance test will be difficult to build or is not obvious.

???

You, the customer, aren't a technical person, but you are responsible for executable Acceptance Tests.

• It is easy to lose requirements when many of them are revealed in the process of questions to the **Onsite Customer**. There are a lot of questions, since there is no comprehensive documentation driving the developer's work.

• We want **Executable Tests**, but the customer is usually ill suited to create them herself.

• Testing is a specialized skill and it is helpful to have professional help, both in doing it and in spreading the knowledge of its requirements. See **Customer-Tester Pair**.

• If no-one captures the answer to a question or a detail of a requirement, it may get lost as the project evolves, but ASD doesn't depend on comprehensive documentation.

! ! !

Therefore, *the customer (or an aide) should create a special test card to specify a test when she answers a question from a developer*. The card can be used later (not a lot later) in a discussion with another person tasked with creating the actual test. Like other cards in agile projects, it is a promise to have a conversation that will nail down a requirement.

• Test Cards need to be turned quickly into **Executable Tests**.

• Close collaboration between the customer and acceptance test developer is assumed here. The tester needs to go back to the customer to validate that the test really is what was wanted.

• Tools such as FIT/FitNesse enable some customers to develop their own tests, but even here, some "glue code" (fixture code) is needed.

• The customer likely needs a team of helpers to assist in the many required tasks [16]. A tester is a key component. **Customer-Tester Pair** is essential in distributed agile development but helpful in all situations in which the customer is less technical.

Acceptance Tests

You are customer on an agile development team. Developers have come to you with a question, or you have just written a new story that you want to give high priority.

???

You want to be able to deploy the software soon after the end of a release, but you need high confidence that it meets the requirements.

• Typical post testing, while still necessary in most organizations, gives you feedback on defects and miscommunication too late to effectively take advantage of it.

• Small errors are less disruptive than larger ones. A small number of errors are less disruptive than a large number.

! ! !

Therefore, *develop executable Acceptance Tests as you go.* The Acceptance Tests, when passing, give the customer assurance that the team has built what was really wanted.

• There should be one or more tests for each story.

• There should be one or more tests for each question answered by the customer.

• Tests for low priority stories can be delayed as long as you note that they have been.

• Note that unit tests only test that the team builds what it thinks it was supposed to build, not what the customer thinks should be built.

• Acceptance Tests guide the developers in the fulfillment of the task itself. Since it is executable, developers code until the tests pass. Then they are done. This avoids over-building.

• Ideally, a complete set of Acceptance Tests should be available for each story at the point it appears in an iteration backlog.

• The **Product Owner** owns the Acceptance Tests.

Note that stories are written and estimated before they appear in an iteration. In fact, some stories may never appear. It is probably still valuable to write at least some of the Acceptance Tests early on, as they solidify the requirement for everyone. In effect, they are an executable specification.

Tools are becoming available for customer readable, even writable, Acceptance Tests.

FIT: http://fit.c2.com/
FitNesse: http://fitnesse.org/
EasyAccept: http://easyaccept.org/

Informative Workspace (Visible Project Tracker)

You are any member of an agile development team. You want to assure that you are aware of progress and impediments to progress.

???

When things are changing, it can be difficult to know where the team is. But many people need to know how things are going.

• All the stakeholders have a need and a right to know the current state of the project with enough detail that they can plan.

• The developers need to assure that complexity doesn't let key issues fall into the cracks.

• Information that needs to be searched for is less likely to be found.

• Risks should be made obvious to the **Whole Team**.

! ! !

Therefore, *create a workspace (physical or virtual) in which all of the needed information is immediately accessible. Preferably it is "in your face."*

• For a co-located team, *Big Charts* are helpful. These include Scrum's *Burn Down Chart*, for example. Just hang simple graphics on the wall.

• Pinning the story cards to the wall, with separate sections for those completed and those under development can be a big help. Have cards of previous iterations on the wall in separate sections.

• Obstacles should have a special, visible, place. They are also noted in the daily **Stand Up Meeting**.

• In general, don't depend on sophisticated tracking tools for this. **Cards and Whiteboards** may be best. They are useless if someone needs to go find them, but might not know where to look.

• This will be especially difficult, but especially necessary, in a dispersed team. Dispersed teams need to compromise here, using tools, but they pay a price. See **Virtual Workspace**.

See Information Radiators [6]

Note: "In your face" is a phrase that implies that information is put in front of you automatically, rather than you needing to go seek it out.

Just Do It

You are a developer on an agile team. You are **Pair Programming** building a feature. You suddenly recognize that you have alternatives for implementation of the current story.

???

You must choose between alternative ways to build something. It seems like a difficult choice as the alternatives have different costs and benefits.

- There are many ways to do any given thing.
- Different solutions have different costs and benefits.
- You want to **Deliver Customer Value.**
- Things may change in the future. Therefore any decision you make now could later prove incorrect.

! ! !

Therefore, *don't obsess over the decision. Pick a simple alternative and go with it.* If something better is found to be needed later, you can change this when doing **Constant Refactoring**.

- Don't forget to **DTSTTCPW**, of course.
- In general, we don't build general or sophisticated solutions. We look for simple design and simple implementation. But don't just hack.
- If things change you haven't wasted resources in overbuilding this feature. In particular, don't build infrastructure speculatively, thinking that it will amortize over future work. If things change, the effort is wasted. This is an extremely difficult lesson for traditionally trained developers who are used to building general solutions and building "helpful" scaffolding at the beginning of a project. "Just say no." Pick a **Simple Design** that doesn't require scaffolding.
- On the other hand, in certain circumstances, you must produce that scaffolding to support sophisticated solutions. Scaling and security constraints come to mind. DTSTTCPW does not imply ignoring information or real needs. Just don't anticipate that it will be needed until the story for it appears in an iteration.

Shrinking Teams

You are an agile team and you are at a point at which your velocity is increasing. Things have apparently been going well.

???

Your team members have increasingly valuable skills that the organization needs to leverage in the best way.

• Once a team gets in the groove, its velocity may increase.

• The skills associated with agile development have value elsewhere in the organization.

• Unless final delivery is especially urgent, the team may be more efficient than it needs to be.

! ! !

Therefore, *split the team or send some members off to found other teams*. This increases agility in the organization overall.

• The current project should get along just fine.

• You can also add a member or two to the original team (**Grow Up**) as a means of training others.

A combination of this pattern with **Think Small** and **Grow Up** is a fundamental strategy for large projects.

But, don't just give the team and its members extra tasks. Remember **One Project**.

Ten Minute Build

You are a developer. You have discovered that **Continuous Integration** is getting harder as you wait for the system to build while incorporating new stories. .

???

If the build takes too long you will tend to integrate less often. Then you find that things don't integrate at all due to drift, requiring you to make major changes.

• If the build is easy and fast, it can be done frequently

• If you don't do **Continuous Integration**, different pairs will build things that don't work together well and you will find this out later rather than sooner.

• During the build, all unit tests are run, and they must all pass.

! ! !

Therefore, *do enough optimization (just enough) so that the system will build in ten minutes.*

• **Constant Refactoring** is used to improve the design and optimize it for build time.

• In extreme cases you may even need to partition along interfaces so that you only need to rebuild a portion of the application for almost all changes.

• The build is automated, of course.

My Story

You are a developer on an agile team. You have taken responsibility for a story for this iteration.

???

You have many responsibilities for your story, but without good tracking, the overall iteration effort could fail.

• The person building a story is the best one to know its state of completion.
• Others will pair with you on the story, but the responsibility remains with you.
• You want to finish your story, of course, but the overall plan is more important.
• The **Social Tracker** needs to be able to inform the customer whether more work can be taken on in the iteration, or whether the team has overcommitted.

! ! !

Therefore, *always know whether your story will be finished successfully in the current iteration.*

• **Sustainable Pace** implies that you don't need to kill yourself to finish your story, but you do need to be able to tell the tracker the state of its development. Honestly.
• It is probably better to be conservative in your estimate. If you aren't sure you can complete the task, say so.
• If you honestly know the state of completion, you can ask for help when needed.

Full Communication

You are a member of an agile team. You know something relevant to the project that others may not know.

???

Customers and developers live in completely different worlds. This can be a serious impediment to effective communication.

• Customers and developers drive different vehicles, drink different beverages, etc. As Martin, Noble, and Biddle like to say, "Customers are from Venus. Developers are from Mars."[16]

• Sometimes customers have options that they don't communicate to developers. This tends to bind the developers if they don't think there are any alternatives.

• Sometimes developers have knowledge of technical opportunities that might accrue if the requirements were slightly different. If they are not communicated, the customer might miss out on being able to take advantage of them.

• It is, to the author, surprisingly common for customers and developers to consciously withhold information from the other. This is dysfunctional.

! ! !

Therefore, *never hold back any relevant fact.*

• Of course, you don't always think to say something that you believe to be obvious. Too often it is obvious only because of your own background that is not shared by the other. This therefore takes special discipline.

• Eventually the developer and customer will become more familiar with each other's world view, constraints, etc.

• The most important thing to say, of course, is the thing that it is most uncomfortable to say. Delivering bad news, when necessary, is valuable. Reward it.

• A simple form of this is to **Offer Alternatives**.

Infrastructure

You are the **Sheltering Manager** of an agile team. It is now the very beginning of the development process.

???

*Agile development depends on a certain set of tools and infrastructure to allow the team to **Deliver Customer Value** in each iteration.*

• Your team has habits. Hopefully most of them are good, but, perhaps, not well attuned to the agile way.

• The practices, such as **Test First** development and **Constant Integration** depend on having tools in place.

• The workspace itself is a key success factor to permit ease of communication and full Information.

! ! !

Therefore, *commit resources to set up the initial workspace infrastructure before you begin development.*

• Pay attention to the physical set up of the developer/customer space.

• You will need a test framework, perhaps a specialized one.

• You will need a code management system that enables integration and testing.

• Don't overdo this. As usual, you want just enough and just in time. But testing and integration, at least, need to happen from the first iteration.

• And don't spend time thrashing around trying to figure out what you need. Sometimes the first iteration itself will tell you that if you pay attention to what difficulties you have with the various practices. An **Effective Coach** can help here, as can a **Retrospective**.

Note that this pattern is not about requirements driven scaffolding for the product. It is just about the basic tools needed so that the team can begin.

High Discipline

You are a developer on an agile team. Development is proceeding. Perhaps you are coding a task.

???

Agile is harder than you think, especially at the beginning.

- No set of practices will pay you any benefits if you don't do them.
- Agile practices are designed to be synergistic and to work together.
- You may not find the practices easy, or even natural, at the beginning.

! ! !

Therefore, *during the initial phase of the project, pay special attention to the practices themselves.* Preferably, record how well you think you are doing them on a numeric scale (in your **Project Diary**, perhaps).

- Once you think you are getting pretty good at them, be sure to evaluate them for effectiveness. Discuss any problems in the **Retrospective**.
- Fall back on the Values and Principles when things seem tough. Understand why you are doing these things. Focus especially on **Delivering Customer Value**.
- The **ScrumMaster** or **Effective Coach** is there to help you achieve this.

Our Space

You are a **Sheltering Manager** of an agile team. Development has not yet begun and you are planning for how the team will work.

???

*People need to **Be Together** in order to work together.* This is more important on agile teams than otherwise.

• People working in cubicles get stuck. It takes effort and time to get unstuck.

• Without comprehensive requirements documentation, the team will depend on communication to settle issues and answer questions. Communication distance is expensive.

• Distractions cost everyone in money and in frustration.

! ! !

Therefore, *provide a space for the team that is organized around maximization of communication within the team. If necessary, use the physical layout to protect them from distractions outside the project.*

• If the team is large or distributed, then Our Space might need to be virtual, rather than physical. This can be made to work, but you pay a price for it.

• The team needs to own the space. They need to be able to modify it as they see fit. Ideally the room will radiate information, though it may not seem "business-like."

• Experience has shown that an open space layout, with room for pairs to work, room for the customer, and room in which to hold a daily standup, just works. This is considered fundamental in XP.

See the patterns for dispersed and distributed development when this is not possible.

Team Continuity

You are a **Sheltering Manager** for an agile team. You have many personnel decisions to make over the life of the project.

???

Most of the knowledge about an agile project is in the heads of the participants.

• The agile team doesn't have comprehensive documentation to fall back on. The code and the personnel are where the key facts are.

• Within reason, people work best when they don't have too many things to concentrate on.

• The people are your chief asset on an agile project. Developers are not interchangeable units of production. Likewise the customer knows better than anyone about strategic decisions that have been taken to date.

! ! !

Therefore, *as much as possible, keep the personnel on the team stable.*

• You can add personnel at a modest rate as you go. But don't lose anyone if you can help it.

• Projection planning, based on velocity, depends on a stable team.

• Eventually, you may be able to use **Shrinking Teams**.

Relative Estimates

You are a developer on an agile team. You are estimating stories and tasks.

???

The more precise your estimates are, the more they cost you to prepare, but the more likely they are to be wrong.

• You can spend a lot of time and effort getting estimates "right," but that doesn't **Deliver Customer Value**.

• Stakeholders need to be able to project estimated costs into the foreseeable future.

• At the beginning of a project you are still tentative about the requirements. Trying to give precise estimates of things that will likely change wastes resources.

! ! !

Therefore, *give relative, not absolute, estimates of the stories.* A story that seems twice as hard as one you did recently gets twice as many story points.

• There is a lot of pressure at the beginning of a project to do precise estimates. Try to resist this. Meaningful numbers will come in a few weeks if the developers spend their time developing (rather than estimating). Once the team velocity stabilizes, anyone can simply project how many story points can be built per iteration.

• It should ideally take less than ten minutes to estimate a story. If it can't be done that fast, you don't understand it, and need to **Spike**. Alternatively, the customer needs to split the story.

• Estimates should be accurate, but not necessarily precise.

• Of course, small things are easier to estimate than large things. Therefore, small stories help. You can partition larger stories into tasks and estimate those.

Half A Loaf

You are setting up a team and hope to achieve the benefits of agile development. You see various institutional impediments to doing everything suggested here and in the literature.

???

Agile development requires a lot of discipline and perhaps a culture change in many organizations.

• An engineering process like XP depends on synergy between the practices to get all of the benefits.

• But some of the practices may conflict with corporate culture.

• However, the practices themselves are good practices. Each has some benefits, even without the others.

! ! !

Therefore, *if you can't do it all, do what you can*. Evaluate what you do, and discuss it at a **Retrospective**.

• You can add practices after seeing how the ones you are doing work out. Doing something like **Promiscuous Programming** might give you the confidence to try **Test First**, for example.

• The goal is to **Deliver Customer Value**, not to please the authors of some book (even a good book.)

Nano-Project

You are organizing a new project, perhaps taking a manager role or technical lead. You have many stakeholders, some of whom are not yet convinced that agile will work for them, or how they will achieve the necessary level of control over the project.

???

A key stakeholder who is unsure of how the new process will work for them can prevent the start of the project.

• Stakeholders often are comfortable with a planned methodology, even when they know it won't work for them.

• Stakeholders have legitimate concerns about how their money will be spent and what they will get in return. Planned development gives them at least the illusion of knowing where they are. They understand PERT charts and the like.

• A small project can show the benefits of agile development quite quickly if carefully managed.

• If this is the first agile project for this team, the developers need a way to learn and practice new skills.

! ! !

Therefore, *under the guise of training, run a very short project using small stories from the real project.* Pay special attention to velocity and tracking. The project can last for a couple of weeks and must deliver real functionality to the hesitant stakeholder.

• The small project can be as short as a couple of weeks, with two day iterations and two **Retrospectives**. Select small stories and train the customer to write such small stories as you go. You could even have **Stand Up Meetings** twice a day.

• You will want an **Effective Coach** or **ScrumMaster** to guide this project on a day to day basis.

• Focus especially on getting a good and a stable velocity in the project and show the stakeholder how it is used to make projections over a set of stories.

• Of course you may also learn that agile is not for your team and stakeholders.

• To truly fulfill the training role, pay attention to all of the practices: testing, integration, etc.

• You will have to readjust your thinking about story size and estimates when you start the bigger project of course, due to the different time scale.

• **Deliver Customer Value** to at least one stakeholder.

Also see **Just Start**.

Personal Velocity

You are a developer on an agile team.

???

You need to know how much work you can do in an iteration so that you can contribute to estimation.

• If the developers don't know individually how much they can accomplish it is harder to make estimates.

• Guessing how good you are isn't likely to be effective. But there are simple ways for you to know how much you can do on the average.

! ! !

Therefore, *know precisely how much work you can do in an iteration*. The **Project Diary** helps you keep records of past work.

• Individual estimates are too variable to be a management tool.

• List stories you have worked on for this project and their estimated and actual time requirements. From this record, you can establish your own velocity.

• Note that personal velocities cannot be compared between team members or even for a single person working on different projects. There are too many variables. The biggest variable is how the individual feels about estimation: optimistic (bad things seldom occur), or pessimistic ("oh dear, we are doomed!")

Offer Alternatives

You are a member of an agile team. You are part of a discussion between customer and developer, playing either of these roles.

???

Something you know may be vital to the success of the project in the short or long term, but others may not also know this, as their background and training is likely different from yours. This is especially true in the case of the different backgrounds of customers and developers.

• Customers and developers sometimes take one another too literally.
• Usually there is a range of acceptable solutions for the customer.
• Usually there are many technical alternatives known to the developer.
• But customers and developers have different training and world views. They even drink different beverages and drive different automobiles.
• Everyone needs to know what is needed and what is possible.

! ! !

Therefore, *both customers and developers need to Offer Alternatives to the other whenever they are recognized.*
• Customers can give the developers a range of possibilities on acceptable requirements in many cases. This can start a conversation on the trade-offs on cost and functionality.
• Developers can recognize that a particular feature is high cost and may be nearly as effective as one of lower cost. Or alternatively, that a small increase in cost could result in a larger increase in functionality.
• **Full Communication** goes beyond the advice given here.

This writer is amazed at the frequency with which a team of developers hides possible alternatives and opportunities from customers. He is likewise amazed at the frequency with which customers withhold from developers what their real needs are, as opposed to their mere desires. Both of these result in inflexibility, poor quality, and high cost.

The customer asks for blue widgets. Blue widgets may cost 50. The developer may realize that green widgets may cost only 30 and the customer may not actually care. This needs to be brought out in discussions about the stories.

Beyond Extreme (Extreme Discipline)

You are a member of an agile team. Success of the team is important to you. But there is some special circumstance making this project especially difficult. Perhaps it is dispersed. Perhaps the stakeholders don't understand the need of users very well.

???

Discipline is needed at every turn. *Without frequent feedback on your process it will be more difficult to maintain discipline and the practices.*

• Many of the agile practices seem, at first glance, to be impossible to perform across distance.

• Discipline is required in any agile project, but especially across distance.

• Feedback, and the subsequent adjustment, are essential in difficult situations.

• *Many of the agile practices, while good, are hard to maintain over distance and many time-zones.*

! ! !

Therefore, *push all of the practices to their limit.* For example, use especially short iterations. Write even more Acceptance Tests, have very frequent **Retrospectives**. etc.

• This requires both clear planning and an understanding of the practices at a relatively deep level.

• Note that as a general rule, the more uncertainty in the project for whatever reason, the shorter the iterations and releases should be. This gives you more frequent feedback.

• Think short iterations, very small releases, single project, single codebase, single build, small team, Whole Team, etc.

This pattern applies in any especially difficult situation, not just dispersed development.

Agility in Large Systems

It is easiest to run an agile project in a small team. However, that isn't always possible. What can you do to maintain agility and scale to large projects?

Think Small

You are a member of a team that needs to build a large system. You want to achieve at least some of the benefits of agile development. You might also be a key stakeholder of such a system, or a manager with wide responsibility.

???

Large systems are hard to build and development efforts often fail.

• Many (most) large systems began life as a small system that grew to its eventual size and complexity.

• Small systems can be built with small, co-located teams.

• Stakeholders may have good insight into the essential need (or not).

• A small system that fulfills an important need can give you time to develop the larger system.

• Requirements for large systems are often bloated.

! ! !

Therefore, *begin with the small, essential, project inside the larger one you think you need*. Then grow from there if necessary.

• As you grow the application you can **Grow Up** the team.

Thanks to Ward Cunningham for this essential insight.

Scrum of Scrums

You are an overall manager of a large agile project composed of many teams. You want to keep the teams coordinated.

???

Several teams working simultaneously on a single project need frequent checkpointing and coordination.

• Several teams can go off the rails if their efforts diverge.

• In general, a team's **ScrumMaster** (or **Effective Coach**) should know what is going on in an individual team. They also have responsibility for process.

! ! !

Therefore, *ScrumMasters hold a periodic (daily) coordination meeting.* Like the daily **Stand Up Meeting** of an individual team, it is to report progress and bottlenecks, not to solve every issue.

• If possible hold this after the daily meetings of the teams.

• Cross team issues can be addressed back in the teams with **Face Time**, **Ambassadors** and the like.

Grow Up

You are one of the key people responsible for the overall success of a large project. You want to achieve some of the benefits of agile development. You have applied **Think Small** to get started. But the current team can't work fast enough to reach deadlines using its **Sustainable Pace**.

???

A small team can only do so much, no matter how much skill and domain knowledge they have.

- People can be introduced into a project using **Pair Programming**.
- You don't want to have the productivity decline while training newcomers.
- You want to maintain a **Humane Workplace** and encourage **Energized Work.**

! ! !

Therefore, *grow a single team slowly by adding a new member or two each iteration for a while until the team is slightly too big.* The newcomers **Pair Program** with the original members to integrate into the project.

- A team can grow from four or so, to a dozen or so this way without losing pace.
- Even a new hire can be productive in Pairing when they act as navigator. In fact, they often bring a fresh perspective that aids the original team.

Once the team is working well split it into two teams, with some of the newcomers and some of the original members. See **Shrinking Teams**.

Interfaces Are Just Another Story

You are a member of an agile team. You must coordinate with one or more other teams on some minimal interface so that you can henceforth work independently on some item.

???

Interfaces between teams need to be negotiated and made concrete so that each team can progress on the common work.

• Teams coordinate best if loosely coupled via negotiated interfaces.
• It takes time and effort to create interfaces.

! ! !

Therefore, *schedule the work on interfaces like any other story in the backlog*. The two teams meeting at the interface will coordinate during some iteration on building this story.

• Use **Ambassador** or **Face Time** to make this work. Otherwise you can use **Remote Pairing** with a member of each team.

Architecture Sprint

You are planning the first iteration of a large agile project.

???

You will eventually have many teams that need to coordinate around a common idea or a common architecture. *Inter-team coordination is difficult and expensive.*

- Complex architecture may best be done by experts.
- Large systems may require some overall framework to guide everyone.

! ! !

Therefore, *consider making your first iteration strictly for building an initial architecture with which the teams can work*. Spend time considering alternatives and remember to keep it flexible.

- The teams can **Grow Up** around this architecture. They will use it as the basis of their **Guiding Metaphor**.
- **But**, communication with, and delivering value to, the customer is more important than adhering to the architecture. So, be prepared to evolve this architecture like everything else.

128

Agility in Dispersed Development Teams

For what ever reason, it may not be possible to co-locate your team(s). While co-location of small teams is the agile sweet spot, it is possible to add additional practices to compensate for the ones that don't work here.

Distributed development will be taken to mean that there are several co-located teams at different locations. Thus each team works together. In contrast, *dispersed* development implies that a single team has members at distinct locations. They might only be as far away as different floor in the same building, or they might be on separate continents.

Large systems generally depend on at least distributed development and the teams may be dispersed as well. But even a small team may be dispersed.

These patterns do not discuss traditional *offshore* development where the management and stakeholders are on one continent and the developers on another. I have little faith in it and believe better solutions exist.

Local Manager

You are forming a highly distributed agile team. It will cover several work sites, perhaps spread over several continents. You have a free hand in setting the management structure for the project (otherwise, see **Single Point Organization**).

???

Distributed development, whether agile or not, has special needs. In particular, people remote from the company center can feel isolated, less valued, and out of the loop. *Team members at all the various sites need to feel connected to the **Whole Team** and the whole enterprise.*

• Many issues arise over the course of a project that are related to things other than the project work itself: pay, conflict, vacations, personal emergencies, etc.
   • Some issues can only be resolved with local involvement.
   • The agile manager is a **Sheltering Manager**. This requires a local view.
   • **Cultural Awareness** is very important in a widely distributed team.

! ! !

Therefore, *organize the project so that everyone answers primarily to a manager at the same physical location.* Local managers assure that corporate policy is correctly interpreted in terms of the local culture. They serve as **Sheltering Manager** for their local team members.

The Local Managers have frequent **All Manager Scrums** to coordinate work and assure that the local part of the team integrates smoothly into the whole.

• The various site managers must all be "on board" for the project and the agile development methodology. If you have been careful to **Train Everyone** and have periodic **Face Time**, it will help.

• Local Managers increase cost and complexity, of course, as the project will require several managers.

• It will be especially important that the Local Manager permit **Self Organizing Teams**, otherwise management can actually get in the way of the work. All of the advice given here to management must be honored by the Local Manager. This is doubly important if the teams are also dispersed.

• But, see **Single Point Organization** for situations in which it is not possible to apply this pattern.

Kickoff

You are managing a distributed and/or dispersed agile team. It is time for the team to begin work on the project.

???

You need the team to work as a unified organism, with trust in each other, yet they normally work at widely dispersed sites and have, perhaps, never met.

• If the team is new to agile development you need to **Train Everyone**. This is expensive if done remotely or via traveling trainers.

• If the team has never worked together, it will be necessary to build trust (**Bonding**). **Face Time** can help do this if it is well planned.

• Early misunderstandings among team members are expensive later.

! ! !

Therefore, *bring everyone together for a period of time at the beginning so that they can meet and begin to build trust.* **Train Everyone** as needed at the Kickoff.

• If you can segue into a **Grow Out** process, so much the better.

• Bringing a team together at the beginning is expensive and it may be disruptive to other work.

• Use the Kickoff as an opportunity for **Bonding**. This may require some funding for social activities. Cooperative games of various kinds can aid in this team formation process.

Source: See Braithwaite et. al. [5]

Also see: Coplien and Harrison [8]: Face to Face Before Working Remotely

All Manager Scrum

You are collectively the site managers of a distributed agile project or you are the overall project manager. You have responsibility for team members at the various sites.

???

Keeping everyone moving in the same direction at the same pace is difficult in a distributed project.

• Managers at different sites need to coordinate. It is just as difficult for them as for everyone else.

• Managers normally have many duties so communication across sites needs to be efficient.

! ! !

Therefore, *have periodic (daily to weekly) manager scrums to coordinate activities and resources.* Each manager should know what has happened since the last scrum, what will occur between now and the next one, and what obstacles prevent smooth movement.

• A real-time scrum, while difficult to arrange, will maximize effectiveness as it permits rapid targeting and removal of obstacles.

• As with any other scrum, the purpose is not to solve all problems, but to locate them. Correction can go offline.

• Time-box the meeting. Don't try to solve every problem in the scrum. It is enough to decide who will address the problem.

• The customer and developers at each site will have daily **Stand Up Meetings** as usual and there should also be a daily **Scrum of Scrums** to coordinate between the sites. .

It is best if the scrum is held in real-time, but you may be successful with a non-synchronous scrum (email, for example, or a wiki) but all must participate. However you try it initially, address its effectiveness in an early **Retrospective**.

Virtual Workspace

You are a member of a dispersed agile team, perhaps the one responsible for setting up necessary infrastructure, though this can be shared by all.

???

Agile development depends on intense personal communication. However, such continuous and intense interaction is very difficult across space and time.

• Communication distance is expensive.

• If you can't "be" together, you can't "work" together.

• Agile development depends on interpersonal communication at all levels at all times. There is no complete documentation to tell you what to do next.

• The less frequently you communicate the more likely it is that people at different sites will diverge in work product and in overall project view.

• It is especially difficult to keep everything visible (**Informative Workspace**) over distance and time-zones.

! ! !

Therefore, *provide a special virtual "home" for the team in cyberspace.* This can be a wiki or use other technology, but it must be accessible and updatable by all.

• All of the team's necessary artifacts should be accessible through this "home".

• The workspace must have a rich set of communication tools, both for instant communication and for preservation and availability of artifacts.

• You will need to simulate **Cards and Whiteboards** and other information radiators in a virtual space.

• Some information needs to be "in your face." See **Informative Workspace**.

Source: See Braithwaite et. al.: Virtual Shared Locations [5].

Multiple Communication Modes

You are a member of a distributed and/or dispersed agile team who must communicate effectively with other members at the same site as well as at other sites.

???

There are many different kinds of communication that must occur in an agile project, but time differences and distance will inhibit all of them.

• If members find obstacles to communication, they will become isolated. The press of other duties will push them to work alone.

• People normally communicate both synchronously and asynchronously, face to face and remotely, etc.

• Communication distance is expensive in agile development as you don't have a lot of prepared documentation to work from.

• In face-to-face communication we have multiple modes of communication: visual, sound, body language, shared experience, etc.

! ! !

Therefore, *provide many different modes of communication*: wikis, mailing lists, web sites, phone, instant messaging, video conference, social media, and **Face Time**.

• Keeping different modes consistent will be a challenge. Don't ignore the difficulty, and make sure that you know what is authoritative when there is divergence.

• Different modes are better at some things and worse at others. A wiki can maintain shared documents. A mailing list is good for quick coordination. Twitter or something similar can be used for emergency communication.

• When you need to know something, you need to know where to look for it. This will also be a complicating factor unless you have a plan for how the different modes will be used.

Make communication a frequent topic at your **Retrospectives**.

Source: See Braithwaite et. al. [5]

Shorten The Path

You are managing a dispersed agile team. Or, you are its **ScrumMaster** or its coach.

???

Communication distance is expensive.

• People need to **Be Together** to work together. But physical distance isn't the main factor.
 • We have evolved for face to face communication.
 • We use various technological tools to help us when **Face Time** is not possible.
 • Bandwidth costs money.
 • So does disruption and miscommunication.

! ! !

Therefore, *shorten the communication distance between team members in any way possible.*
 • Many of the patterns here, such as **Face Time**, speak to this.
 • Be prepared for the cost.

Note that there is a cost to communication distance no matter what you do. Small co-located teams are ideal for agile development. If you must use people separately located (even by as much as one floor in a building) you will pay a price. You can use money to mitigate this by buying bandwidth to connect your people. But the cost of bandwidth plus reduced efficiency will probably still be more that the cost of having people co-located. So make sure that you have excellent reasons for dispersed teams.

There are excellent reasons. Companies like IBM and Schlumberger have a philosophy that everyone in the company has an equal part to play. They realize this with teams that cross all sorts of boundaries: cultural, national, etc. They are willing to pay a price for this unification of the company. It isn't the low cost solution, however.

Presence Indicator

You are one of the key members of a dispersed agile team, In Scrum terminology, you are one of the pigs . Your team members are distributed around the country or the world. Actually, they might just be on another floor in your same building.

???

It isn't necessarily clear who you can interact with right now. Who can answer your questions? Who is available for remote pairing?

• In co-located agile development, all you need to do is raise your head to see who is in the room. In distributed development, you want to achieve the same ease of knowing who is available.

! ! !

Therefore, *provide a way for everyone else's presence to be obvious to you when they are available*. For example, if all of the key people, including the customer, have a special instant messaging account to which they log-in, then everyone else can add them to their buddy list.

• Whatever mechanism you use needs to be as simple as possible to use so that it does get used. Adding your name to a wiki page when you come in, probably won't work as it requires too much discipline to keep it up to the minute accurate.

• Specialized communication clients can provide this Presence Indicator, perhaps as a list of small iconic avatars in a toolbar.

Source: See Schümmer and Schümmer [19],

Grow Out

You are managing a distributed agile team at its inception and wonder how best to organize the overall project over its lifecycle.

???

Agile development depends on a Community of Trust [8] and intense communication. This is best achieved in a co-located team, and will be inhibited by distance.

• Communication distance is expensive in agile development.
• Travel and personal disruption are also expensive.
• Especially at the beginning, the team must build trust to work effectively.
• Early misunderstandings can cost a lot later.

! ! !

Therefore, *begin the development (one or two iterations, say) with everyone co-located.* Then move the members back to their ordinary work sites.

• This is expensive, of course.
• If the project will also grow to a large size, see **Grow Up** also.
• You may be able to begin with a co-located small team whose members represent the various sites. The team grows when they go back to their normal locations.
• This technique will aid **Bonding** and increase trust. If the team is to be long-lived the added initial expense may be well worth it.

Customer-Tester Pair

You are a member of a dispersed agile team in which the customer is remote from the developers.

???

Likely the customer has a lot of business knowledge and speaks with a business appropriate vocabulary. Likewise the developers have technological knowledge and speak the language of technology. These are not the same language. *If you try to separate the customer from the rest of the **Whole Team**, communication will fail as the developers and the customer speak different languages.*

• Sometimes co-location of customer and developer is impossible. This is expensive.

• You need to prevent any and all communication barriers between the customer and the rest of the team.

• **Acceptance Tests** are understandable by the developers and can guide their development. They can also assure that they **DTSTTCPW**.

• **Acceptance Tests** are understandable by the customer (or at least by analysts) and can serve as executable specifications.

• In general, separating the customer from the developers is expensive and dangerous in an agile team. You need to spend a lot of effort to compensate for this.

! ! !

Therefore, *co-locate the **Onsite Customer** and an acceptance tester*. The acceptance tester is a developer who will specialize in capturing the requirements as **Executable Tests** on behalf of the customer, making them available to the rest of the team who may be located remotely.

• The acceptance tester here is an especially important example of an **Ambassador**.

• This may be less expensive than moving the customer to the developers or moving the developers to the customer.

• The acceptance tester in this role can rotate and doing so will spread knowledge, though at an added travel and accommodation expense.

An especially productive form of this is the Customer Team [16] composed of customer, tester, analyst, political advisor, infrastructure guru, etc.

Be Together

You are a member of a dispersed agile team. There are others with whom you must work. They may or not be at the same site.

???

If you can't Be Together you can't work together.

• Working in different time zones makes communication difficult.
• An answer may not be available when you need it.
• Waiting for an answer or a decision is expensive.
• Developers making up requirements or making incorrect assumptions is expensive.

! ! !

Therefore, *organize daily schedules so as to maximize the amount of time you are working simultaneously.* This will be disruptive everywhere, but will enable communication.

• The disruption is not just to the business, but also to the lives of the team members.
• Managers will need to find ways to compensate members for this disruption. Otherwise it will be impossible to achieve **Energized Work**. The compensation must be valued by the team members.
• A several hour time difference can be split between the team components with some working earlier and some later in the day.
• An organization with a culture of flex hours will find this difficult, though it also makes agile development in general difficult.

See **Shorten The Path.**

Face Time

You are a manager responsible for organizing a distributed agile team and making it effective.

???

Agile depends on a Community of Trust [8]. *Trust is hard to develop and maintain over distance if the members only rarely meet.*

• People work best face to face.
• Sometimes fifteen minutes together can be more effective than a week communicating remotely.

! ! !

Therefore, *schedule periodic visits between (at least) the **Customer-Tester Pair** and the rest of the core developers.*

• Bringing many people together is probably expensive. It may also be disruptive. You probably don't need the **Whole Team** at any give soirée, however.
• Face Time should be used for **Bonding** as well as the work product.

I have seen teams who were spread over only a few miles, but who seldom met, solve many irritating problems quickly given a bit of Face Time.

Source: See Braithwaite et. al.: Visits Build Trust [5]

Ambassador

You are a member of a distributed agile team. Different skills are located at different sites, but not all skills are available at each site.

???

The classic problem of developer-customer miscommunication is magnified by distance. Other skills may be needed somewhere but available only elsewhere. *You need to effectively bring the expertise to bear where it is needed.*

• On a distributed project your expertise may not be immediately available where it is most needed.

! ! !

Therefore, *send someone with a special skill to the location where it is needed whenever needed.* The Ambassador will keep the team moving, but will also, over time, spread the skill to others.

• The threshold for "whenever needed" is adjustable. If you must err, do so on the side of too much early in the team's development. Otherwise the project can go off the rails through ineffective action.

• It is hard to make the travel time productive, however. So short, frequent, stints are probably worse than fewer, longer ones.

The acceptance tester in the **Customer-Tester Pair** is a permanent Ambassador whenever the customer must be distant from the remainder of the team.

Source: See Braithwaite et. al. [5]

Remote Pair

You are a developer on a dispersed agile project. Perhaps the other developers are also dispersed. Perhaps not, but there is someone at another site who has knowledge needed here or who needs knowledge available only here.

???

Pairing is a core practice of XP and is considered so by many other agilists. *Without pairing, the other practices will be very difficult to maintain*: **Collective Ownership**, **Constant Refactoring**, etc.

• Pairing, a key agile practice, is especially challenging across distance and time-zones.

• Pairing is synergistic with most other practices, such as **Collective Ownership**, **Constant Refactoring**, etc.

! ! !

Therefore, *use internet tools to pair remotely*.

• High discipline will be required, especially initially, to maintain this practice. You may have to go **Beyond Extreme**.

• Periodic **Face Time** is also helpful in building the trust that enables this remote pairing.

Find and use tools with low bandwidth requirements so that you can also maintain **Multiple Communication Modes**.

Source: See Braithwaite et. al. [5]

Single Point Organization

You are a top-level manager of a distributed agile project at the point of defining the overall organization of the team. You have decided that **Local Manager** is not appropriate.

???

In a distributed team there can often be confusion about how decisions are made. This can become frustrating for everyone.

• Confused management reporting lines will cause disruption, as it will be difficult to maintain a coherent message across sites.

! ! !

Therefore, *provide a simple reporting structure. At each level of the organization authority resides in a single person only.* If team members must report to managers at a different site, they must have individual local managers to provide them support.

• Assure that the management structure is clearly communicated to everyone and that everyone knows her role in the overall project plan.

• But, use **Self-Organizing Team**s to maintain agility.

Source: See Hvatum et. al. [10]

Feature Focused Teams

You are organizing a distributed and/or dispersed agile development. You have flexibility in placing personnel.

???

Since your team isn't in one location, your skills inventory is dispersed. *You need to organize your people for maximum effectiveness.*

• Communication distance is expensive in agile development. This is exacerbated if people at different sites must coordinate closely on the creation of any artifact such as the code.

• Organizing by skill (skill based groups) guarantees that when different skills are needed to build a story, the communication must cross site boundaries.

• Organizing by phase of the project guarantees that the product must move to a new "skill site" leaving the expertise at that point behind.

! ! !

Therefore, *organize the sites so that each of them is a complete agile development team that is focused on feature development for the customer.* Each site will have members with all necessary skills for the development of features at that site.

• A customer feature then tends to stay at one site.

• The **Whole Team** then has several skills available.

Rapid Response Teams

You are a top-level manager for a distributed agile team at the point of defining the overall organizational structure of the team. The skills of your team members are not distributed in such a way that you can easily use **Feature Focused Teams** that are also **Whole Teams**.

???

Whenever questions occur in an agile project they must be answered by some person as there is little or no base documentation to work from. *If questions are not answered in a (very) timely manor, individuals, perhaps the entire team, may be blocked.*

• Many questions that arise cross disciplines and areas of expertise. Everyone needs a clear source from which to extract definitive answers.

• It may not be possible to have each area of expertise represented at each site.

! ! !

Therefore, *design a team support structure so that each required skill can be quickly brought to bear wherever needed.* For example, put the people on the various feature teams who have the most database expertise on a special database support team. This team can assist other teams who lack this skill on an as needed basis, perhaps as **Ambassadors**. *Most individuals are on more than one team and have more than one responsibility.*

Don't conclude from this that, for example, the Tester Team is the one primarily responsible for tests. They provide test expertise that is utilized by everyone, so their members are primarily part of **Feature Focused Teams** teams as needed. The same is true of all specialist teams.

• Don't let these "teams" detract from the unity of the **Whole Team**.

• For a different solution see Balanced Sites in [5].

Each person may be a member of several of these sub-teams. Some, such as the acceptance tester in the **Customer-Tester Pair**, certainly are.

Source: See Hvatum et. al.: Communication Strategy[10]

Cultural Awareness

You are a manager of a widely distributed and/or dispersed agile team, or a member of the organization's Human Relations department, or even a member of a team who must interact with members who come from different cultures than your own.

???

People from different parts of the world have different customs and expectations of professional interactions. *Cultural differences can cause especially strong barriers to effective communication, as they are often overlooked.*

• People have most experience interacting with others much like themselves.

• Cultural differences may be hard to notice and therefore hard to overcome and compensate for.

• A deep knowledge of cultural expectations and mores is often necessary. This deep knowledge is not common to the technical groups.

! ! !

Therefore, *pay special attention to cultural factors*. The literature can help, as can an effective Human Relations department. Make sure that everyone understands the possible conflicts. Have someone in the organization ready to do training as needed. This might be especially useful when you **Train Everyone**.

• You may need a trained observer, especially at a **Retrospective**.

• **Face Time** can be an effective time to resolve difficulties. An **Ambassador** can also help.

In my personal practice I have seen a dramatic instance of this when a multi-national team was brought together for the **Kickoff**. Initially there was little interaction until **Bonding** exercises were used.

Source: See Hvatum et. al. [10]

Bonding

You are managing a distributed agile team and are developing a budget for the medium-long term.

???

Agile development depends on a Community of Trust [8]. Trust is difficult to maintain unless it has personal as well as professional aspects.

• Agile development is a team activity. It should not be possible for individuals to succeed while the team fails.

• Commitment to the project is necessary, but also commitment to the team itself.

! ! !

Therefore, *establish a budget for social activities*. The activities are to be determined and scheduled by the **Whole Team**. Some of this should be spent during periodic **Face Time**.

• Some of this is cheap and easy, but some is not.

• Training exercises can contain elements if social interaction.

• Don't let institutional barriers become an obstacle. Build a better workplace if necessary to be effective. In some institutions a certain amount of subterfuge may be required. But even that can build camaraderie.

Source: See Hvatum et. al.: Social Funds [10]

Some Speculation

 Here are some "patterns" that we aren't quite so sure about. They may work for you. They may work in special situations. They are presented here not necessarily as expert advice, but to encourage you to think beyond what you normally consider. They arose from discussions with people, including Kent Back, who think deeply about these things.

Daily Deployment

 You are an agile team in a highly competitive business environment. Your software has a lot of users.

???

 Competition demands that you rapidly enhance your product and this demand is constant.

- Small changes can be deployed instantly if disruption can be minimized.
- Your competition is trying to best you.
- You want a close relationship with your most enthusiastic users.

! ! !

 Therefore, *deploy new features daily*. As soon as a new feature is available, tested, and integrated, deploy it.

- Build a deployment cycle that rolls out small changes to users immediately.
- Successful companies such as Google do this, of course.
- It may demand rolling out changes to a few customers so that errors don't affect all your users.
- Be prepared to roll back unwise updates. Make this part of your update cycle.

Pay Per Use

You are in a situation in which your customer sees some benefits of a proposal, but is hesitant to commit to it.

???

You need a revenue stream to further development, but no one seems to want to commit to a project.

• Development costs money.
• It is easier to generate funds when you are already providing a benefit.
• A key customer might be willing to help you guide the development of a product if they can do so with little up-front cost and an increasing benefit stream.

! ! !

Therefore, *write a contract with the customer that will pay you per use of the system*. Take on the risk of failure and share in the success.

• You can adjust the rate of pay to the sophistication of the product, so that as you move from release to release the rate of payment increases. Thus the customer will get good value at every point.

Clusters of Patterns of Agile Practice

In any pattern language there are clusters of patterns that work together and reinforce one another. In particular, no single pattern is likely to completely resolve all of its forces. Therefore, other, smaller scale, patterns are applied to help resolve the remaining forces.

Clusters may help explain the synergy between the practices. Here is one that contains many of the patterns in this collection and is centered on a key pattern.

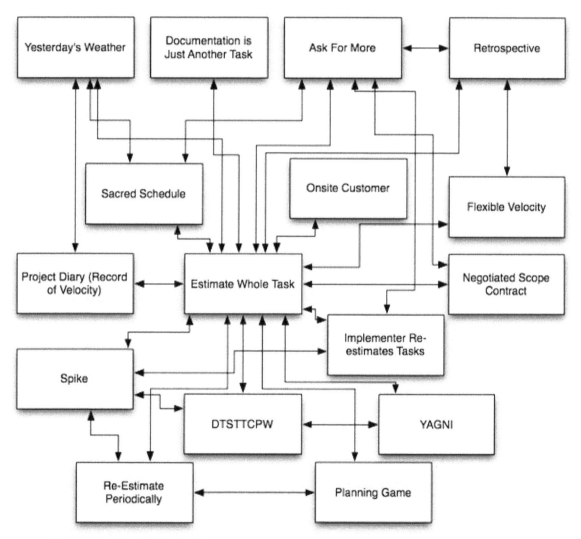

Estimate Whole Task Cluster

The central pattern in this group both reinforces and is reinforced by the other patterns here. For example, we **Estimate Whole Task** because we need enough time for **Documentation**. On the other hand, the **Implementer Re-estimates Tasks** precisely to give us enough time. Likewise, in finding enough time to do rich and complex things we need to **DTSTTCPW** to achieve it or we will not be able to end the iteration successfully. **Retrospectives** help us refine our practices when we find difficulties generally, and especially with time. And when we have set aside too much time, we can and do **Ask For More**.

Note that there are some complex interconnections here, and also note that the patterns seemingly at the periphery are themselves richly connected to other patterns in this language.

Likewise the cluster for dispersed agile development is very complex. The number of these interconnections implies a high level of synergy among these patterns.

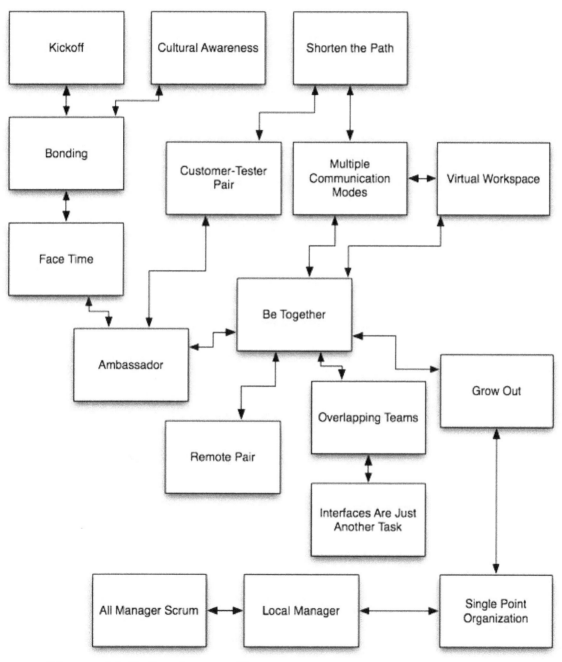

Dispersed Agile Development Cluster

The large system development cluster shows a few connections among the specialized patterns only. Since large system development is necessarily dispersed to a greater or lesser extent, those patterns help here also, of course.

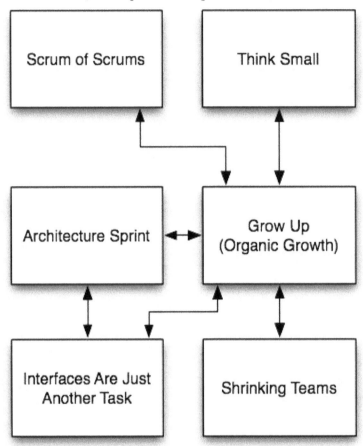

Large System Development Cluster

Advice For Managers

Many of the patterns here speak directly to those tasked with managing an agile team or an agile organization. The most important of these are **Sheltering Manager** and **Self-Organizing Team.** Once you have a working team, you shouldn't need to do much other than remove obstacles from their path.

A consequence of **Collective Responsibility** in the team, however is that the rewards should also be shared among team members. When it comes time to reward the team, let them decide how to partition rewards. On the other side, we don't need to spend time and effort partitioning blame when things go wrong. Instead, we just have the **Product Owner** write a new story to make things right and then schedule it as desired. Only **Stories** move the project forward.

In organizations just getting started with agility, especially those with a long history of doing things in other ways, there may be great reluctance to begin. Too many managers want guarantees that change won't come back to bite them. I have seen projects fail because important managers dithered while deadlines approached, wanting guarantees that things would go well. This occurred even though the manager had no confidence in the standard methodology of the organization for this project. In this case, you have to **Just Start**. You can also try a **Nano-Project**. Try anything to move forward toward your goal. Note that you don't need to commit millions initially. If you commit enough for an iteration or two (a few weeks), you will learn important lessons and your team will gain some skill.

In organizations starting out, don't forget to **Train Everyone** and to bring on board an experienced **ScrumMaster** or **Effective Coach**. And don't neglect to have (and attend) **Retrospectives**.

For a large and important project, don't forget to **Think Small** at the beginning and then let the team **Grow Up** as you begin to advance.

You can track your team quite effectively using the team's velocity once it stabilizes. If you have a fairly good backlog of stories for the project and most of them have been estimated in story points, you can use the team's velocity to project quite accurately how long it will take the team to complete any given amount of work. You need to be a few iterations into the project to do this, of course. So, while traditional projects would be gathering a comprehensive set of requirements and developing an overall design, the agile team is making progress in approximately the right direction. If the traditional team is wrong, much work needs to be discarded and redone. If the agile team is wrong, they just re-steer by writing new stories and continuing as usual.

On the other hand, you cannot use velocity to compare teams or individuals, or even two projects done by the same team. There is too much variation between teams and projects for this to be meaningful at all. Some of the variables involve how the customer thinks about the features (hence their granularity), whether the team members are optimistic or pessimistic estimators, the difficulty of the project work itself, etc.

Remember that in agile development we don't try to over-specify projects. The main variables are scope, cost, schedule, and quality. if you try to specify them all, you will fail, and usually everything slips. In agile development scope is the dependent variable. We specify the others, and do what can be done within those constraints. But we always **Deliver Customer Value** and build **High Value First**. Then the features that slip off the end have low value to the stakeholders. See **Negotiated Scope Contract.**

Advice For Customers

The role of **Onsite Customer** or **Product Owner** is well known to be the hardest job in an agile project. You will get a lot of questions and quick and accurate answers are essential to the progress of the developers. It will impact your productivity off the project so be prepared for it. Ideally, you will have few other duties than working within this team. However, it is still a lot of work for just one person. The work of Martin et. al. [16] is especially helpful. They develop the idea of a Customer Support Team (see **Customer-Tester Pair**).

You will need to write stories and maintain the backlog of stories. You will need to prioritize them based on both the needs of the (many) stakeholders and the costs as represented by the story estimates. You need to select stories for the next iteration and the next release. Keep in mind it is always **High Value First**. Your participation in the **Planning Game** is essential.

Beyond that you need to provide executable **Acceptance Tests** for each story and for each question you answer. You will need to verify that each story is done as it is developed and complain if it doesn't meet your needs.

On the other hand, you are allowed to ask for change at the start of any iteration for any reason whatever. If things aren't to your liking, either because things weren't built as you would like or because needs change, just write another story and schedule it into some upcoming iteration. No problem. No blame. Stories scheduled into iterations are what move you forward. Nothing else does.

Your job is hard because you need to coordinate all the needs of all the stakeholders. The team should seek and get advice only from you. This keeps them working well (if the answers come promptly) and also gives you fine grained control over what is done.

And make sure your views get represented in the **Retrospectives**. While the developers on the team have complete control over how they work, you have the last say in what is built. If you see things not working, discuss it with the **ScrumMaster** or **Effective Coach**. You are a member of the team, not its manager. But you are a full member.

It will be good if you seek the advice of the developers on alternatives to things you want. They may have some ideas about cheaper or better ways to achieve a goal that you may not be aware of, but don't forget that you are the final referee on what is to be built. But to get there, you often need to express the intent surrounding a feature, not just the feature itself. An example (begun in **Self-Organizing Team**) from the military might be useful. A Marine commander might tell a squad to "Go take that hill." Many lives might be lost in doing that, when the intention is really just to get intelligence about what is on the other side of the hill. Had the intent been made clear, the squad might have been able to achieve that more simply. In fact, the military does try to act exactly in this manner.

Since the team's velocity is the primary means of knowing how much you will be able to accomplish. be ready when they **Ask For More** but also respond appropriately when they need a **Graceful Retreat**. **Don't Push Too Hard** or your velocity number will get skewed, making it less useful. A stable velocity is your main tool for projecting schedule and cost.

And of course you really need to be **Onsite**. If you are not, then the team will get stalled and your costs will go up. The only real alternative to being onsite (fully available with quick response to questions) is to go back to something resembling waterfall with complete up-front requirements. This reduces the possibility of change and drives up the cost of change and flexibility.

Advice For Developers

Most of the patterns here are intended to keep you on track. But the big success factor in agility is discipline. Of course, no methodology works if you don't actually execute it. Agility isn't an excuse for hacking or being negligent. Development is hard work.

On the other hand, you have a right to a **Humane Workplace (Be Human)**. You shouldn't have to work 50 hours a week, and you shouldn't kid yourself that it doesn't have serious consequences to do so. Companies that demand it (either from the top or from workers themselves) are, in my opinion, dysfunctional. Agile development practice assumes that software development is intelligent work, requiring skill and knowledge. It isn't "coding." It is creating.

On the third hand, **Energized Work** can be exhilarating. It can be fun to go to work and to interact with your colleagues. All it takes is cooperation of a few people and a single **Sheltering Manager**. The first XP project ran mostly under the radar in a large organization. If you want to get started with ASD, you can also try a **Nano-Project** within your own group to get a feel for the process and for its institutional fit.

Don't make assumptions about the stories. Ask the **Onsite Customer**. If you don't get a quick answer, move on to some other task until it arrives.

But don't neglect **Retrospectives** in which you really look at what happened and formally capture what worked (so that you can repeat it) and what didn't.

And it goes without saying that you need a high level of skill in the basic tradecraft. You need to be able to create beautiful, even poetic, code. You need deep understanding of the basic paradigms of programming, whether they be functional, imperative, or object-oriented. There is no way to win with ugly, funky, manky code.

Finally, when things get tough, fall back on the principles in the Agile Manifesto. Being agile doesn't mean following a defined set of practices faithfully and without thought. It means finding out what works for your team and doing a lot of that.

Getting Started With Agile Development

Here I will assume that you are an experienced organization in developing software, but you currently use more traditional processes. You have heard about agile development and wonder if it is right for you.

My own consulting practice deals mostly with people in just this situation. My first advice, even before I start you charge you, is this: If your current process works for you, use it. If you have high confidence that your current process will succeed on whatever project you are contemplating, you don't need to talk to me, or anyone like me.

However, if you believe, or have evidence, that your own process is failing or likely to fail, agile development likely has something valuable for you, especially on a critical project.

The "sweet spot" of agile development is a small to medium size, but important, project (say under 10 person-years) in which there is uncertainty of any kind. The uncertainty could center around what you want, or what the market needs, or changing technology, or doubt about your own process. Uncertainty makes planning difficult or impossible. When you can't plan, build on tight feedback loops. This is agile.

I particularly like a project in which it is impossible, even in principle, to know all of the requirements before you start. The feedback from **Small Releases** is then essential to know what direction you should take. Steering the project is then like riding a bicycle over rough ground, keeping your eye on the big goal, but able to change when necessary.

In your first agile project you want to learn as much as possible and end up with valuable organizational skills. To do this requires commitment to the project and this is only likely to occur if the project is something meaningful and valuable. A project can be small, but it should be something you really need, even mission-critical.

You will need to understand that of the four major variables of development (features, cost, schedule, and quality), agile development controls all except features. Features (scope) is the dependent variable here. An agile team undertakes to build as much as can be sensibly done under constraints of money, time, and quality. Too many processes fail because they try to control all variables and find at the end that all have slipped: it is late; it costs too much, it performs badly, and we didn't really build everything anyway.

The way that agile development wins while leaving scope undefined, is to have a team work closely and continuously with a stakeholder representative to build the desired features in roughly "value" order.

To get started, you need a **Sheltering Manager** and either an experienced **ScrumMaster** or an **Effective Coach**. Likely you will need to hire someone for the latter role, or take on a consultant. Part of the job of the consultant, over the course of a project, is to train someone in the organization to fulfill that role. You will also need someone in the organization to act as **Onsite Customer**. This person will need deep domain knowledge and be well-connected to the stakeholders. You won't need to commit a lot of resources to the first project, since the project will work in short iterations and may be cancelled at any time. However, the customer role is a full time endeavor.

You should likely use Scrum as your overall management strategy for the project and some well-defined day-to-day process within the Scrum Framework. Many organizations start out with XP, at least until they learn what is best over several iterations. It is important to take all of whatever process you start with, rather than selecting pieces, because of synergies. Thus, everything in XP except **Pair Programming**, for example, doesn't work very well unless you supplement with other practices. But you need experience to know what they might be. Before you reject a practice, be sure that you know how to do it correctly. Target difficulties in **Retrospectives**, and try to improve your practice before changing it. Only then will you know what really works for you and what doesn't.

Once you have the three key people in place, form a **Whole Team**, **Train Everyone** and **Just Start**. Watch the process to see what it gives you at what cost. Many organizations have been pleasantly surprised. In particular, **Pairing** doesn't drive up cost as you might think. **Test First** doesn't slow you down. But this assumes that you use **High Discipline** and perform all of the key activities.

How Agility Wins

Agile software development has a lot to offer to organizations building important software whether as a product or to support something else.

Suppose you could reach your markets more quickly with better quality products. Suppose you could reduce the cost of the software and reduce the amount of bloat and cruft in it. Suppose you could build a happier and more cohesive workforce. Would you do it? Lies, all lies, you may think, but the practices of agile software development can lead to these outcomes.

Agile organizations reach their markets quickly by using short iterations and **Small Releases**. This puts your product in front of real users, but also gives you feedback on the outcome early in the process when you can still change direction if necessary. **Test First** with **Executable Tests** means that quality issues show up immediately, when the results can improve the product, rather than at the end of a long development, when they can't.

Cost can be decreased by considering the following facts. First, we build **High Value First**, so that the most important features are guaranteed to get early attention, while at the other end, if you watch the cost per feature curves, you can cancel when you realize you are only building low value features. Furthermore by using **Simple Design** and **DTSTTCPW** implementations, we don't pay for scaffolding until it is really needed, possibly delaying expensive decisions. In particular, you maximize value by maximizing the quantity of "things not built."

Test First also reduces cost, though it is a bit subtle. If developers follow the mantra of *no code without a failing test,* then they won't build things speculatively thinking they "might" be needed in future. Such anticipatory extensions add to the maintenance cost and increase the likelihood of error in the future, as they make the code more complex. Failing unit tests tell you immediately that you have a problem, when you are still thinking about the issues, rather than later, when you need to recreate the thought processes around the code that is failing. Therefore the team is less likely to get stuck, to get stuck on smaller issues, and to recover more quickly when they do get stuck. **Pair Programming** also helps here, since when the driver gets stuck the navigator can bring a fresh perspective. It is much less likely that both will be stuck at the same spot.

You also win with agile software development by reducing the cost of change. In fact, in today's world, any methodology that makes change expensive must fail. The cost of change in an agile process is precisely the cost of a new story; a new feature. If it isn't right, or if you don't like it, for any reason, write a story and schedule it into a sprint.

Finally, the process as a whole leads to a **Humane Workplace** by maximizing human interactions in the process and providing **Energized Work** and **Self-Organizing Teams**, and insisting on a **Sustainable Pace**.

One thing you should keep in mind is that agile development won't guarantee that you are never disappointed. In fact, you will be disappointed often, but with small, easily recoverable, disappointments, rather than a gigantic one at the end of a project when all is lost. Small disappointments occur when a team has to ask for a **Graceful Retreat**, or when it builds something other than what the **Onsite Customer** wants. We don't try to spread blame in this case. After all, this is usually caused by a shared miscommunication. The customer desires something. Therefore, she asks for something, which might not exactly match what was desired. On the other hand, the developers were asked for something and they built something, which may not be exactly not what was asked for. Finally, when the team builds something and the customer looks at it, she may realize that the original desire wasn't really the right thing anyway. All of these result in disappointment. Time was spent unproductively. Rather than blame someone, just write new **Stories** and move forward. Iterations are short so you can recover gracefully. Blame only reduces everyone's sense of self worth, and ultimately your productivity.

In the long term, there are a number of big wins in using ASD. A **Humane Workplace** with happy, creative, people is big. Having **Executable Tests** for everything eases all of your future maintenance. Owning a process that lets you easily respond to change and build in the face of uncertainty is enormous. **Energized Work** in **Self-Organizing Teams** is an enriching human experience. Hard work can even turn out to be enjoyable. Amazing.

Additional Resources

Cautionary Stories
Brooks, *The Mythical Man-Month: Essays on Software Engineering, Anniversary Edition* (2nd Edition), Addison-Wesley, 1995

Dispersed and Distributed Development
Eckstein, *Agile Software Development with Distributed Teams*, Dorset House, 2010

Large Systems
Eckstein, *Agile Software Development in the Large*, Dorset House, 2004
Larman, Vodde, *Scaling Lean & Agile Development*, Addison-Wesley, 2009

Pairing
Williams, Kessler, *Pair Programming Illuminated*, Addison-Wesley, 2003

Planning
Beck, Fowler, *Planning Extreme Programming*, Addison-Wesley, 2001

Refactoring
Fowler, *Refactoring: Improving the Design of Existing Code*, Addison-Wesley, 1999

Retrospectives
Derby, Larsen, *Agile Retrospectives*, Pragmatic Bookshelf, 2006

Stories
Cohn, *User Stories Applied*, Addison-Wesley, 2004

Testing
Crispin, House, *Testing Extreme Programming*, Addison-Wesley, 2003
Meszaros, *xUnit Test Patterns*, Addison-Wesley, 2007
Rainsberger, *JUnit Recipes*, Manning, 2005

Training
Bergin, Extreme Construction Training Exercise,
http://www.youtube.com/watch?v=_xEp7x4vDqk

Acknowledgements

Linda Rising was the most able shepherdess of several of these patterns for EuroPLoP 2006. As always her advice is helpful, drawing as it does on her deep knowledge of both patterns and topic. I thank her profusely. In 2005, James Noble shepherded several others and gave great encouragement for this project. Several other patterns were workshopped in various PLoPs. The participants have all been very helpful and we thank them. They include, but are not limited to the following people: Neil Harrison, Frank Buschmann, Andy Longshaw, Andreas Rüping, Kevlin Henney, Markus Völter, and Didi Schütz.

Fred Grossman is my colleague and fellow agile trainer and coach. Together we have learned a lot. Ken Schwaber and Jim Coplien got me started with Scrum. Kent Beck and Ron Jeffries disabused me of many early misconceptions about XP. I thank them all.

Thumbnails

This section includes short descriptions of all the patterns we have identified to date. Slight variations on these names are used in the text to elicit the ideas. Some of the alternate names (given in parentheses here) are used interchangeably.

Acceptance Tests. Create a suite of Executable Tests that will be sufficient for the customer to accept the work. They are under control of the customer.

All Manager Scrum. (distributed project) Site managers have a frequent coordination meeting.

Ambassador. [5] (distributed project) A representative of a needed skill group visits the remote team.

Architecture Sprint. (large project) In a sufficiently large/complex project, it may be necessary to have an initial iteration that sets a starting overall architecture for the system. This architecture may need to evolve over time so simplicity here is a virtue as elsewhere.

Ask For More. When you know you will have extra time within an iteration, ask the customer for more work.

Be Human (Humane Workplace). Provide a Humane Workplace to maximize productivity.

Be Together. (distributed project) Adjust time schedules to overlap in time as much as possible.

Best Effort. The contract is not for features delivered on a given date. You want Best Effort and full communication.

Beyond Extreme. (distributed project, primarily) Push all practices to their most disciplined point.

Bonding. (distributed project) Provide funds for social bonding within the team.

Bug Generates Test. When a bug appears in code, write a set of tests that will only pass when it is corrected.

Cards and Whiteboards. Things change too frequently to depend on elaborate documentation mechanisms.

Coding Standard. Everyone shares the same coding look and feel.

Collective Ownership. The team as a whole owns all of the created artifacts, especially the code.

Collective Responsibility. The team shares responsibility and rewards for all tasks.

Common Development Environment. [10] All developers use a common platform and agreed tools.

Constant Refactoring. The structure of the code is continuously improved to take account of all stories built to date.

Continuous Integration. Every task is integrated at completion and all unit tests are made to pass.

Cultural Awareness. [10] (distributed project) Develop resources to overcome cultural differences.

Customer Checks-Off Tasks. Only the customer knows when something is done.

Customer Obtains Consensus. The customer role is responsible for obtaining consensus among the stakeholders.

Customer-Tester Pair. (distributed project) The customer works at one location with an acceptance tester.

Daily Deployment. (tentative) Deploy new features daily.

Daily Scrum. See Stand Up Meeting.

Deliver Customer Value. Building things may be fun or not, but don't lose track of the real reason we are doing this.

Documentation Is Just Another Task. Every story requires some kind of documentation. If it must be extensive, include it in estimates.

DTSTTCPW. Do the Simplest Thing that Could Possibly Work. Build the code to implement the story and nothing more. Pay for generality only when you know you need it.

Easy Does It (Don't Push Too Hard). As a customer, don't push too hard. It frustrates everyone. If you push too hard and "win," you lose if the iteration doesn't complete successfully.

Effective Coach. A novice team depends fundamentally on a coach (ScrumMaster) to keep you to the discipline and help you see opportunities and problems.

End To End. The first release is an end to end version of the product.

Energized Work. Sustainable Pace. Management sets work conditions so that everyone can work at their optimum over extended periods. E.g. Forty Hour Workweek.

Estimate Whole Task. Estimates must include everything necessary for a story.

Executable Tests. Tests are run so frequently they must be executable.

Face Time. (distributed project) Schedule time for significant parts of the team to work periodically on one site, especially the customer and developers.

Feature Focused Teams. (distributed project primarily) Create teams around the features, not according to skill types.

Flexible Velocity. Use velocity to allow for needed work that is not in the stories. But learn to get it into the stories.

Full Communication. The developers keep the customer apprised always of opportunities, costs, difficulties, etc. The customer keeps the developers in the loop on the business needs and thinking that may affect future directions.

Graceful Retreat. When you have overcommitted to an iteration, the customer chooses the work to complete.

Grow Out. (distributed project) The team begins co-located for an iteration or two.

Grow Up. Start with a small team and grow it to the required size by adding a few developers at iteration points. The other practices enable this: Promiscuous Programming…

Guiding Metaphor (**Topos**). Develop a guiding metaphor or story for the project that guides people as to the general direction.

Half A Loaf. If the team is new and there is resistance to the practices, try the ones you think will give you the most benefit and then review in a Retrospective. Consider adding more practices as you go.

High Discipline. No methodology will succeed if you don't actually do its practices faithfully. On the other hand, make sure they are the right practices or deal with the issue in a Retrospective.

High Value First. Customer selects highest value features at every point.

Humane Workplace. See **Be Human**.

Implementer Re-estimates Tasks. Tasks are best estimated by the person who will do the work.

Individual Stakeholder Budgets. When customer representatives can't come to a common understanding of priorities, they may need individual budgets of team resources.

Informative Workspace. The team room (Our Space) employs Information Radiators so that progress and impediments are visible to any visitor. Whiteboards, note boards, etc., need to have enough graphically displayed information that anyone can immediately see the progress of the current iteration as well as any bottlenecks.

Infrastructure. Before the project begins make sure the basic build, test, integrate, deploy infrastructure is in place.

Initial Velocity. The initial velocity, measured in story points, is a small fraction of what you estimate it is possible to do in the first iteration. Thereafter, it is just **Yesterday's Weather**.

Interfaces Are Just Another Story. (large project) If teams must coordinate over interfaces, write a high priority story to define the interface.

Just Do It. When faced with choices that are all feasible, just pick one and do it.

Just Start. Rather than talking and talking about how to do the project, just start it.

Kickoff. [5] (distributed project) Begin the project with a face to face meeting lasting some days.

Local Manager. (distributed project) Everyone has a manager local to their own site.

Multiple Communication Modes. (distributed project, primarily) Provide many modes of communication and high bandwidth if the team can't share much **Face Time**.

My Story. Know the state of progress of the story you are working on.

Nano-Project. (large project, usually) A tiny project can quickly show the benefits of agile development to a reluctant stakeholder.

Negotiated Scope Contract. Scope is the dependent variable in an agile project, so plan for this when you write your development contracts.

Offer Alternatives. Developers Offer Alternatives to Customers when they recognize them. Conversely, customers Offer Alternatives on desired features to developers to get feedback on likely costs and consequences.

Once And Only Once. [2] Refactor code so that everything is said only once. But pay for generality only when you must.

One Project. Everyone works on only one project at a time.

Onsite Customer (Product Owner). The customer works in the team's room along with the rest of the Whole Team. Communication distance is very expensive.

Our Space. The Whole Team works together in an open workspace to optimize communication.

Pair Programming. No code is committed to the code base unless it is written by a pair.

Pay Per Use. (tentative). Write a contract with the customer that will pay you per use of the system. Take on the risk of failure and share in the success.

Personal Velocity. Each developer knows how much work she can do in an iteration. The Project Diary helps her keep records of past work. Individual estimates are too variable to be a management tool.

Planning Game (Sprint Planning Meeting). Once each iteration (every two weeks, say) the team spends time planning the iteration, including what stories will be immediately built. See the literature as this is a highly disciplined planning exercise.

Presence Indicator. (distributed project) Provide a way for everyone else's presence to be obvious to you when they are available.

Product Owner. See Onsite Customer.

Project Diary. Each developer keeps a bound book for the project. It is private to the individual and contains things like estimates vs. actuals on stories built, who you paired with, ideas for the next Retrospective, etc.

Promiscuous Programming. Spread the knowledge of the project amongst the team members.

Question Implies Acceptance Test. When the customer answers a question from the developers, she captures the answer in an acceptance test.

Rapid Response Teams. (distributed project) Provide a matrix of skilled people to assist teams.

Re-estimate Periodically. Things change and estimates become obsolete.

Relative Estimates. Estimate quickly into a small number of estimation "bins." Don't spend time to be more precise than necessary in estimation.

Remote Pair [5] (distributed project) Find the tools to pair remotely and do it consistently.

Retrospective. Periodically hold a retrospective [14] of the team's practices.

Sacred Schedule. Time never slips in agile development. Features are the dependent variable.

Scrum of Scrums. (large project) ScrumMasters hold a periodic (daily) coordination meeting.

ScrumMaster. The ScrumMaster is responsible for process and for removing obstacles.

Self-Organizing Team. The team is responsible for its own internal process, practices, and management.

Sheltering Manager. A new team will depend on some shelter from those in the organization who don't readily accept change.

Shorten The Path. Shorten the communication distance between team members in any way possible.

Shrinking Teams. If team velocity is increasing it may be possible to shrink the team and maintain sufficient velocity. Those freed can initiate other projects.

Simple Design. Design only for the current stories. Simple logic, minimal generality, pass the tests.

Single Point Organization. [10] (distributed project) Everyone has a single reporting manager, and if that manager is at another site, a local manager to provide support.

Small Releases (Incremental Development). Software is released on short cycles, say monthly.

Social Tracker. The tracker must know how everyone is doing.

Spike. Do quick prototypes to learn how to build or estimate something.

Sprint. Iterations should be very short. A week to a month. Iterations deliver business value as determined by the Onsite Customer. They are strictly time-boxed.

Stand Up Meeting (Daily Scrum). Fifteen minutes every day, to keep everyone on the same page.

Stories (Product Backlog). All work is captured on story cards that form the basis of estimation, scheduling, and projection.

Sustainable Pace (40 hour week). Pace the team for the long haul, not a sprint. You want everyone working in top form all the time.

Team Continuity. Management commits to keeping the team together throughout the project. Team members make a similar commitment.

Team Owns Individual Velocities. Individual velocities are not a management tool.

Ten Minute Build. Do enough optimization (just enough) so that the system will build in ten minutes.

Test Card. If the customer cannot write executable tests herself, then she creates Test Cards in answer to each question. The card specifies an acceptance test that will then be written by the implementer of the story.

Test First. [2] No code without a failing test.

Think Small. (large project) Begin with the small, essential, project inside the larger one you think you need. Then grow from there if necessary. This assumes you start with a small team and grow it if and when necessary. See Grow Up.

Train Everyone. Initial training includes everyone, including customers and management.

Virtual Workspace. (distributed project) Provide a cyberspace home for the team with effective communication tools.

Whole Team. The team includes everyone with an essential skill. In particular, it includes the customer as a full team member.

YAGNI. You Ain't Gonna Need it. Don't anticipate what might not occur. Don't scaffold speculatively.

Yesterday's Weather. The velocity of the next iteration is exactly the work successfully completed in the previous one. Of course this assumes that the time and personnel are fixed.

References

[1] Alexander, Ishikawa, Silverstein, *A Pattern Language*, Oxford, 1977

[2] Beck, Andres, *Extreme Programming Explained*: 2ed, Addison-Wesley, 2004

[3] Beck, *Smalltalk Best Practice* Patterns, Prentice Hall, 1996

[4] Belshee, Promiscuous Pairing and Beginner's Mind: Embrace Inexperience, http://www.agile2005.org/XR4.pdf

[5] Braithwaite, Joyce, XP Expanded: Distributed Extreme Programming, XP 2005 Proceedings, LNCS 3556, 2005

[6] Cockburn, *Agile Software Development*, Addison Wesley, 2001

[7] Cohn, *Agile Estimating and Planning* (Robert C. Martin Series) Prentice Hall, 2005

[8] Coplien, Harrison, *Patterns for Agile Software Development*, Prentice Hall, 2004

[9] Humphries, *Introduction to the Personal Software Process*, Addison-Wesley, 1997

[10] Hvatum, Simien, Cretoiu, Heliot, Patterns and Advice for Managing Distributed Product Development Teams, EuroPLoP 2005, UVK Universitatsverlag Konstanz GmbH, 2006

[11] Jackson *Principles of Program Design*. Academic Press, London and New York, 1975

[12] Jeffries, Anderson, Hendrickson, *Extreme Programming Installed*, Addison-Wesley, 2001

[13] Kerievsky, *Refactoring to Patterns*, Addison-Wesley, 2005

[14] Kerth, *Project Retrospectives: A Handbook for Team Reviews*, Dorset House, 2001

[15] Manns, Rising, *Fearless Change*, Addison-Wesley, 2004

[16] Martin, Noble, Biddle, "Programmers Are From Mars", Customers Are From Venus. PLoP 2006 proceedings.

[17 Mugridge, Cunningham, *Fit for Developing Software : Framework for Integrated Tests*, Prentice Hall, 2005

[18] Rueping, Agile Documentation : *A Pattern Guide to Producing Lightweight Documents for Software Projects*, Wiley, 2003

[19] Schümmer and Schümmer, "Support for Distributed Teams in Extreme Programming", in Extreme Programming Examined, Succi and Marchesi (eds), Addison-Wesley, 2001

[20] Schwaber, Beedle, *Agile Software Development with Scrum*, Prentice Hall, 2002

[21] Surowiecki, *The Wisdom of Crowds*, Anchor, 2005

[22] Yip, It's Not Just Standing Up: Patterns for daily Stand-up Meetings, PLoP 2006 Conference. Portland, OR, 2006

Index

Acceptance Test...**4**

Acceptance Tests............vi, 8, 9, 16, 39, 41, 42, 68, 69, 76, 82, 105, **106,** 122, 137, 155, 164

All Manager Scrum..vii, 128, **131,** 164

Ambassador....................................vii, 124, 126, 137, **140,** 144, 145, 164

Architecture Sprint...vii, **127,** 164

ASD...**8**

Ask For More............................vi, 9, 23, 31, 34, 38, 46, 55, 56, 73, 78, **90,** 150, 156, 164

Be Human..v, 8, **50,** 63, 157, 164, 166

Be Together..vii, 115, 134, **138,** 164

Best Effort...v, 9, **28,** 48, 97, 99, 164

Beyond Extreme..vii, 30, **122,** 141, 164

Bonding..vii, 130, 136, 139, 145, **146,** 164

Bug Generates Test...**v, 54,** 164

Cards and Whiteboards...vi, 10, **65,** 107, 132, 164

Coding Standard..vi, **88,** 89, 102, 164

Collective Ownership..vi, 88, **89,** 141, 164

Collective Responsibility.......................................v, viii, 9, 24, **43,** 44, 89, 153, 164

Common Development Environment..vi, **102,** 164

Constant Refactoring...........................vi, viii, 44, 75, 88, **94,** 95, 108, 110, 141, 164

Continuous Integration.................................vi, viii, 41, **76,** 77, 110, 165

Cultural Awareness...vii, 128, **145,** 165

Customer...**3**

Customer Checks-Off Tasks...vi, **82,** 165

Customer Obtains Consensus...vi, **84,** 86, 165

Customer-Tester Pair..16, 57, 69, 105, **137,** 139, 140, 144, 155, 165

Daily Deployment...vii, 47, **147,** 165

Daily Scrum...v, 15, **45,** 165, 168

Deliver Customer Value. .v, 31, 34, **37,** 47, 55, 61, 90, 92, 103, 104, 108, 113, 117-119, 154, 165

Do the Simplest Thing That Could Possibly Work...92

Documentation Is Just Another Task..vi, 57, **67,** 165

Don't Push Too Hard...v, **48,** 156, 165

Done...**4**

DTSTTCPW........................vi, 8, 9, 35, 39, 61, 73, 75, **92,** 108, 137, 150, 160, 165

Easy Does It...v, 9, **48,** 165

Effective Coach....v, 8, **13,** 14, 15, 21, 25, 26, 42, 43, 45, 113, 114, 119, 124, 153, 155, 158,

165

End To End...vi, 8, 36, **103,** 165
Energized Work..vi, 24, **97,** 99, 125, 138, 157, 160, 161, 165
Estimate Whole Task......................v, viii, **57,** 59, 61, 67, 71, 73, 74, 79, 82, 149, 150, 165
Executable Tests......................................v, 8, 9, 40, **41,** 42, 67, 105, 137, 160, 161, 164, 165
Extreme Programming...**6**
Face Time.......................vii, 26, 124, 126, 129, 130, 133, 134, **139,** 141, 145, 146, 165, 166
Feature Focused Teams..vii, **143,** 144, 165
Flexible Velocity...vi, 58, 72, **73,** 94, 165
Full Communication..vi, 9, **112,** 121, 165
Graceful Retreat......................................vi, 23, 49, 55, 57, 73, **91,** 156, 161, 165
Grow Out...vii, 130, **136,** 165
Grow Up.................................vii, 23, 109, 123, **125,** 127, 136, 153, 166, 169
Guiding Metaphor..v, 8, **26,** 84, 127, 166
Half A Loaf...vii, **118,** 166
High Discipline...vi, 63, 114, 159, 166
High Value First....................................v, 9, **35,** 37, 96, 154, 155, 160, 166
Humane Workplace......................................v, **50,** 100, 125, 157, 160, 161, 164, 166
Implementer Re-estimates Task...**55,** 150, 166
Incremental Design..**87**
Incremental Development...v, **47,** 168
Individual Stakeholder Budgets...vi, 85, **86,** 166
Informative Workspace...vi, 10, 65, 66, 71, **107,** 132, 166
Infrastructure...**113,** 166
Initial Velocity...v, 8, **34,** 38, 166
Interfaces Are Just Another Story...vii, **126,** 166
Iteration..**4**
Just Do It..vi, 61, 92, **108,** 166
Just Start...v, **25,** 119, 153, 159, 166
Kickoff...vii, **130,** 145, 166
Local Manager..vii, **128,** 129, 142, 166
Multiple Communication Modes.....................................vii, **133,** 141, 166
My Story...vi, 100, **111,** 166
Nano-Project...vii, 25, **119,** 153, 157, 167
Negotiated Scope Contract....................................vi, 29, **96,** 154, 167
Offer Alternatives...vii, 112, **121,** 167
Once And Only Once...vi, **75,** 167
One Project...v, **23,** 98, 109, 167
Onsite Customer......1, ii, v, 8, 9, **16,** 18, 26, 30, 32, 38, 46, 47, 69, 78, 82, 90, 91, 103, 105, 137, 155, 157, 158, 161, 167, 168

Our Space...vii, 8, 100, **115,** 166, 167

Pair Programming...3, vi, viii, 40, 44, 55, 60, 63, 64, 88, **100,** 101, 102, 108, 125, 159, 160, 162, 167

Pattern..1

Pay Per Use...vii, **148,** 167

Personal Velocity..vii, 9, **120,** 167

Pigs and Chickens...**6**

Planning Game.............v, 8, 9, 17, 29, **31,** 32, 34, 35, 38, 45, 48, 55, 57, 61, 71-73, 155, 167

Presence Indicator...vii, **135,** 167

Product Backlog...3, v, **32,** 168

Product Owner...**3,** v, **16,** 32, 106, 153, 155, 167

Project Diary.............................vi, 9, 55, 58-60, 63, **80,** 114, 120, 167

Promiscuous Programming...........................vi, **63,** 100, 118, 166, 167

Question Implies Acceptance Test...vi, **69,** 167

Rapid Response Teams..vii, 23, **144,** 167

Re-estimate Periodically..vi, 58, **71,** 167

Refactor...**4,** 36, 40, 42, 52, 54, 57, 71, 73, 87

Relative Estimates...vii, 34, **117,** 167

Release...**4**

Remote Pair...vii, 100, 126, **141,** 168

Retrospective......vi, 9, 21, 24, 31, 34, 46-48, 57, 66, 72, 74, 82, 87, **104,** 113, 114, 118, 119, 122, 131, 133, 145, 150, 153, 155, 157, 159, 162, 166-168, 170

Sacred Schedule...v, **52,** 57, 168

Scrum...**4**

Scrum of Scrums...vii, **124,** 131, 168

ScrumMaster......v, 9, 13, **15,** 25, 31, 43, 45, 46, 78, 114, 119, 124, 134, 153, 155, 158, 165, 168

Self-Organizing Team..v, 11, **24,** 104, 142, 153, 155, 160, 161, 168

Shared Code..**89**

Sheltering Manager....v, 8, **11,** 12, 13, 15, 22, 23, 97, 113, 115, 116, 128, 153, 157, 158, 168

Shorten The Path...vii, **134,** 138, 168

Shrinking Teams...vi, **109,** 116, 125, 168

Simple Design..vi, **87,** 108, 160, 168

Single Point Organization.......................................vii, 128, 129, **142,** 168

Small Releases...v, 37, **47,** 158, 160, 168

Social Tracker.........................vi, 9, 42, 45, 55, 59, 73, **78,** 90, 91, 111, 168

Spike...vi, 9, 55, 57, **61,** 62, 71, 117, 168

Sprint..**4,** v, vii, **30,** 31, 32, 37, 52, 127, 164, 167, 168

Sprint Backlog...4, 32

Sprint Planning Meeting..v, **31,** 167

Stand Up Meeting............................v, 15, **45,** 46, 62, 78, 104, 107, 119, 124, 131, 165, 168
Stories...19, **32,** 155, 168
Story...**3**
Sustainable Pace...vi, 8, 50, 83, **99,** 111, 125, 160, 165, 168
Team Continuity...vii, 23, **116,** 168
Team Owns Individual Velocities...vi, **59,** 168
Ten Minute Build..vi, 41, 76, **110,** 168
Test Card..vi, 69, **105,** 169
Test First...v, 8, **39,** 54, 93, 113, 118, 159, 160, 169
Think Small..vii, 103, 109, **123,** 125, 153, 169
Train Everyone...v, 8, 11, **21,** 129, 130, 145, 153, 159, 169
Unit Test...**4**
Velocity...**4,** 34, 38
Virtual Workspace...107, **132**
Whole Team. v, 8, **19,** 20, 21, 68, 85, 104, 107, 122, 128, 137, 139, 143, 144, 146, 159, 167, 169
YAGNI...vi, 8, 75, **93,** 169
Yesterday's Weather..iii, v, 23, 34, **38,** 49, 52, 60, 82, 94, 166, 169
You Ain't Gonna Need It...93
High Discipline...**114**
XP...**8**

www.ingramcontent.com/pod-product-compliance
Lightning Source LLC
Chambersburg PA
CBHW080414060326

40689CB00019B/4238